TRAITORS
IN OUR
MIDST

By
ANNA

ISBN-13: 979-8-218-09389-1

DEDICATED TO

The people of the world who love freedom.

CHAPTER ONE

Phil pushed the play button on his answering machine when he saw the red blinking light. As the machine turned off, he sat looking at the phone as if a phantom from the past had suddenly appeared. He thought about his boss who wasn't going to believe the call.

He worked at a newspaper as a reporter, and he had his own weekly column that many readers enjoyed. The executives above him insisted on honesty, and his boss, Bob, often returned writeups asking for the author to produce facts that substantiated the story. At one meeting, his boss let everyone know that no one better turn in another story like the one he received the week before, "We do not print opinions. Please keep that in mind whenever you turn in a story. This paper is not going to print trash like most of the other papers that give their readers political opinions and unprofessional ideas to follow when they know nothing about the subject. So I want a complete list of what each of you is working on and the research you're doing to come up with your reporting. We need proof for what we're saying to back up a story if there is ever an accusation of falsehood. Please remember I won't stand for lying to the public."

Phil smiled to himself as he warmed up the leftovers he had from the night before. Yes, his boss had integrity and morals unlike most of the people he knew in and out of business. It was a time of confusion and fear, and the government ensured chaos was rampant. Phil tried to watch political figures more closely, because he believed the unrest was to take the focus off of what the shady politicians were doing.

Finishing his meal quickly, he turned on the nightly news to see what the newscasters were reporting. Phil wondered how the American public could stand to watch the garbage that was reported each day. All they had to do was look around at the world they were living in to see that the media was pushing propaganda to keep people in line.

The next day, he walked in to see his boss. "Hi Bob, how you doing today?"

"Hi Phil," Bob looked up from the article he was reading. "What's up?"

1

"I received a call yesterday from the assistant to retired Congressman Phineous Handler. Seems the old man wants to talk about his past and let the public know a few things."

Bob was silent for a minute and then asked, "Why would he do that? He has to be at death's door."

"I think that may just be why he wants to talk," Phil responded.

"Go see him," Bob said. "Record everything he says if he'll allow it, and also write down his movements, expressions, and any body language he uses. After you go over the conversation and what you've written down, you'll know what to do with it." Phil thanked him for his input and left his office.

Bob stood up and walked over to an old filing cabinet that had been in the corner of his office for years. Flipping through some old narratives that his staff had written for the newspaper, he grabbed a few about Handler and sat down looking back over the years. Bob knew their news reporting days were numbered with the way the country was churning and changing. They would sooner or later be shut down by big government so the regime could control every bit of news the people received.

It always amazed Bob how so many citizens were followers who believed whatever they were told and acted on impulse whenever they were directed to react on an issue by people they didn't even know. "Well," he thought, "the American people went along with government's decisions, at least they had so far. Maybe they wanted the United States to be a third world country where they would have no rights and were managed by a handful of devious leaders who cared nothing for anyone or anything except their personal power and riches." He shrugged and picked up another article he had to review for printing that night.

Phil called Handler's house and set up a meeting for the next day. That night while he ate supper, he sat on his couch writing down a slew of questions he wanted to ask Phineous. He sat back to watch the evening news. They were saying and showing the same things they had for days. Embedding their propaganda into viewers' minds was what Phil called it. Anyone with any sense would never believe what these newscasters said, and he often wondered how the newscasters themselves could say such blatant lies. Did they get paid off or get some other kind of perk for doing this? They had to see a benefit somehow, and the benefit had to make them think their unrealistic reporting was worth it.

He reached over and shut the TV off thinking back over the events he knew caused the nation to spiral downward, but he couldn't help wonder how all of this had actually started. It couldn't have been just random. Maybe Phineous could shed some light on this, or maybe the old man just wanted someone to talk to besides his assistant. For a high-profile man who had been in the public eye for decades, it must be hard to sit and watch the world go by. He didn't trust Handler, but he knew Bob would help him sort out truth from lies. He was more than willing to do any research necessary and then decide how they could get this out to the public if it was indeed fact and not fiction.

The next afternoon, Phil arrived at Handler's house. As he approached the front door, it opened, and he was escorted down a long hall and into the library of the Congressman who summoned him. The reporter noticed that hundreds of books lined the shelves that bordered the room, and it wasn't lost on Phil that books the retired Congressman had written were setting on a table by the couch.

"So you're Phil Bender the reporter for the column 'Facts and Proof'. I like your column," Congressman Handler said looking Phil up and down.

"Thank you," Phil's attention came back to his host, and the reporter extended his hand. Phineous shook his hand, and Phil noticed the old man's grip was still strong even though he looked tired and emaciated. The pictures of Phineous' younger years showed a handsome man, and now the reporter saw that Handler kept his looks even into his eighties.

The retired Congressman motioned for Phil to sit across from him on the plush, beige couch. His host was sitting in a wheelchair but appeared to be alert and attentive to his surroundings and what was being said. He asked Phil if he would like some refreshments before his butler left. His guest declined and got comfortable in his seat.

"I hope you don't mind if my assistant stays. He already knows everything we will discuss, and if I do stumble, he will be able to shed some light on the details."

"That's fine with me," Phil responded nodding at the assistant with a smile. "Do you mind if I record our conversation and take some notes?"

Handler laughed. "No, I don't mind. You see, I know that I have little time left on this earth. So your recording will do me no harm, but perhaps it can help our people. I'm not certain that is possible anymore, but it is worth a try. I am truly ashamed of what I have done and also what many of my colleagues have done. Of course, I know each of us will pay for our transgressions. I am a strong believer in God although for the past sixty years or more have ignored Him and chosen a worldly path. Because of those decisions, I have hurt millions of people without a thought in order to gain my millions and my status. Now the time has come to ask for forgiveness from our people as well as God for all that I have done. No matter what my eternal punishment is, I know I deserve it."

Phil looked at a man who was still very realistic even though thoroughly corrupt. The reporter wondered if Phineous was truly sorry or only getting back at those he had served with in the political world. That question might never be answered, but it was intriguing to at least see what he had to say. Phil believed in God, and he already knew many people in government would have a very rough time once they came face to face with the Savior. Of course, whatever happened at that time was up to God alone.

He set his recorder on the polished table between himself and his host. "Can you tell me how you think the downfall of our nation started? What part did you play?"

Phineous responded, "I'll get to that. This will take some time for us to get through, so I hope you will be able to return as many times as necessary so I can tell you my viewpoint and how I believe it all came about. How do you get here?"

"I walk. It's only a couple of miles, and you know what the current transportation situation is. I can come back as many times as needed," Phil smiled at the old man. "You already know that I will research what you tell me. It will be very hard to use the information we discuss with the current Administration putting those who don't agree with them in jail, but I won't be using any material that is only presented to get even with someone you dealt with anyway."

Handler smiled, "I understand. There were some who were honest and tried to work for their constituents, but I will be discussing the actions I took along with self-loving senators, congresspeople, businesspeople, news moguls, etc. who didn't give a damn about anyone but themselves. Of course, I'm not going to name them. This is about me and the actions I took. If your research brings up the names of the others, so be it. I'm not doing this to incriminate anyone but myself."

"Fair enough," Phil said. "Maybe we should start with how long you were a congressman."

Handler looked through Phil as if he wasn't there, and then he began to reminisce. "I was elected a congressman at the age of twenty-five and stayed in the House for over fifty-five years. Those years were the best of my life, or so I thought." He stopped talking and seemed to be turning the pages of his life remembering events throughout the years. Suddenly he came back to the present, "You know the only mistakes our Founding Fathers made were not making term limits for Congress, the Supreme Court Justices, and all judicial appointees. And, all judges and Supreme Court Justices should be voted in by the people. Of course, the men who planned our democracy had integrity, morals, and religion all of which they believed those who served later would have. Unfortunately, that is not always the case, and I don't know one member of Congress who would risk life or prosperity to ensure the United States remains a free nation."

"Why do you believe the Supreme Court needs term limits?" the reporter asked.

"Well, anyone sitting on the Supreme Court should certainly know what the Constitution and the law says. From my perspective, many of the current and past Justices voted according to their political ideals and not exactly for what the law or Constitution said on some things. Or perhaps they decided not to get involved with a case that truly needed to have Supreme Court oversight. A decade ago, they did the right thing on the abortion issue by sending the decision back to the states. But they refused to hear a case by multiple states on fraudulent elections. That really isn't acceptable, because the High Court was the states' only option for a remedy. The Supreme Court should have heard the case and resolved it according to the Constitution. The Justices have a job just like everyone else, and they need to go by law not personal preferences or not wanting to get involved. Term limits and majority vote approval would be much better," the old man waved his hand as if the subject really didn't need any more discussion.

Changing the subject, Phil encouraged Phineous to go on, "What happened when you first got to Congress? Did you like the other House members? Did you participate in designing laws that were passed?"

"I was thrilled to be in D.C.," the old Congressman said. "Working with the top House members was quite an experience, and I learned a lot. Of course, new members did things the way the older members wanted them done. Anyone who did things their own way was ostracized, and they never really served. No good committee assignments, no opportunity to work closely with others and learn, no invitations to events, and especially no help at election time. The ambitious who focused only on their constituents were like untouchable dead weights and never really accomplished anything. But, being a 'member of the club' brought all desires to fulfillment. When you are intertwined with all the issues, there is no right or left side but only one party that achieves what the members want and damn the people. At least that was the way it was when I served, and from my perspective, it has only gotten worse since my retirement not long ago."

Phil was speechless. He never thought that any politician would own up to the filthy tactics taken to hurt the country he loved. The reporter began to feel contempt for the man sitting in front of him, but being a professional, he disregarded what he was feeling and continued to listen.

Handler looked out the window and asked Phil, "What did you see on your way here?"

"I saw buildings that had been burned or destroyed by vandals, very few people on the street because of the high crime, and two gangs firing weapons from cars. Thankfully I was down the street so they didn't notice me."

Phineous then asked, "What didn't you see?"

The reporter was perplexed and sat there not knowing what to say.

His host answered for him, "You didn't see anyone laughing or smiling. You didn't see kids playing in yards of the ghettos people live in or local schools with playgrounds for the kids. When you pass people, you don't see them smile or nod, because they are watching for anyone who will jump out to rob, beat, or kill them. You see different races and people of lower income levels who have disregarded the law for years and were encouraged by government to hurt, steal, and destroy anything they wanted in the name of reparation and justice. Reparation was a good term used for anyone who wanted to believe they were owed something and could just take without working or trying to improve their life. An entire generation given the idea they could break any law they wanted without repercussions.

Those same people who continue to try those tactics will eventually be put in labor camps out of the public eye never to be heard from again. They aren't owed anything anymore because the government doesn't need them to cause trouble and confusion anymore."

Phil nodded and asked, "What do you see when you look out the window?"

"I see just what the officials wanted and intended," Phineous said without smiling. "We are in the end stages of their plan. Obedience to a government that cares nothing about people. Anyone who is in their late twenties or older can compare now to a few decades ago and see that we have lost the greatest country in the world. Now, in 2030, we are a socialist country on the verge of communism."

The two men sat there looking at each other. Phil just watched Handler instead of asking another question.

The old man started again, "Being part of the in-crowd, I cared for nothing except my own ambitions. You know, to see how rich I could get, how much power I could acquire, and how much status I could attain in our country and others around the world. All of this was accomplished through friendships, acquaintances, and people who were patriotic to no one or nothing. I started looking out for myself as I learned many of the people in Congress focused on subterfuge, so I learned rapidly. The people I watched took perks they could get and lied unashamedly when they felt they had to.

Handler thought for a minute. "So, one of the first things I learned was that I could make people do things. For years I took advantage of my staffers. Either I made them look for more lobbyists who would pay good, or I pushed them into having sex with me. You see, years ago being a staffer was very coveted, so only one or two in all those years turned me down for anything.

7

The staffers who could produce contacts who would give lots of benefits to me were remunerated handsomely. The lobbyists I worked with gave me such things as wonderful trips and contributions to my campaign so I would work on laws that benefited their client's business or advocacy group. Many times, I was slipped great sums of money under the table, and the laws that were wanted by those lobbyists were always passed. Of course, I didn't consider how much the laws actually hurt our country." He paused for a minute, "No one in Congress who was taking bribes thought of that, and look where we are now. Of course, no one called them bribes but awards, small gifts, or donations to good causes.

Those who supplied sex as long as I wanted it were rewarded in different ways. Nothing was beyond consideration for them. Those who refused me were treated brutally, and of course they left. Using people like that never bothered me until I found out a few of the vultures who met my grown daughter tried the same. That was when I discovered how something like that can hurt a person for years."

"Isn't it illegal to accept money from lobbyists and to use the workplace for sexual harassment?" Phil asked the old man with distaste.

"Of course it is. But, did you ever hear of me being prosecuted for breaking the law? No, you didn't. Hardly a person in government is charged with wrong doing unless they are a huge threat to those in Congress, so there were no boundaries, and I did as I pleased. I played their game and had dirt on those who worked around me. That was my insurance."

Phil sat there and shook his head. "All those decades and no conscience at all about the way you sold out your constituents or used your people."

Handler ignored what the reporter had said, "And then there are the laws that I helped get voted through. Most of the time, the regulations passed didn't affect my people directly, so they never felt the pain for a long time. The people who suffered the most were inner city folks. Years ago, the civilian housing projects under Roosevelt's New Deal built housing for white people. Eventually a few projects were built for African Americans in different locations. This started the segregation of housing and was followed by federal and local laws. Of course, some laws were changed over time to stop segregation, but the inner city was still mostly for certain races while the suburbs were for others. That kept racial tension as an option for politicians like me to use when we wanted to separate the people and make some believe they were discriminated against or pinpoint issues for elections.

"So segregation was supposed to stay?" the reporter asked.

"I don't think so initially," Phineous pondered the question. "That was before my time, but it turned into that. I believe the way of the very unscrupulous politician really started when Roosevelt began the New Deal a hundred years ago, which he really did start to benefit the people. Very quickly those in government could see the personal benefit in what Roosevelt had done. Over the following decades the politicians became extremely more corrupt, and government's role increased dramatically in citizens' lives. Many were hired to run the agencies that helped the people, and that was the beginning of the monster regime we have. When the depression was over and our country was back on its feet, the government didn't back off but continued to increase the budgets and develop new programs. Over the time I served, it was easy for me to add things in bills that gave those who paid me what they wanted and also to add things I thought would benefit me in the future. Back then people believed in their representation. Perhaps a program or law was not popular, but certainly the people could trust those in office or so they thought," Handler let out a sinister laugh that reminded Phil of a demon.

Phineous stopped to take a drink. He motioned to his assistant, and his aide brought him the medicine that he was required to take. "I am sorry about this interruption, but when you get to be my age there are times when you must stop for a minute and take care of priorities. This medicine helps me to think more clearly," Handler swallowed the pills.

"Now where was I? Oh yes," the old man regained his train of thought, "people trusting government. A silly concept today, at least for people who think and are realistic, but decades ago that was not the case. And in all honesty, most of the programs back then were started with partly good intentions. By the time I took office, most officials spoke out of both sides of their mouths. Slowly I saw where I could gain more power and status by verbally pushing a bill that was important to the people. Behind the scenes, I was helping whoever didn't want the bill to succeed as well. That way, I could work both sides and make friends everywhere."

"So you never cared about anyone, especially our citizens," Phil started jotting notes down on his tablet.

"No, can't say that I did. When I think about encouraging people over the decades to use public assistance, to not worry about getting a job or getting off of welfare, and ensuring them the government would take care of them I feel regretful. I didn't realize how easy it would be to steer people in that direction and how easy it would be to make laws giving government more and more power. You see for a country to be healthy, all who possibly can must contribute. Too many people think the government magically makes money to support them, and so it comes down to too few people working to support our nation. Add to that the uproars we caused making people believe they were being discriminated against by each other and needed reparations. Then include in that the millions of non-citizens allowed into the country constantly who need to be supported by taxpayers. That is why the spiral to take down our country increased in speed.

We also have to look at the composition of our country's people. To stay a healthy nation, we must have a solid citizen base and band together. Politicians destroyed that with illegal immigration, insisting on abortion on demand, making certain drugs were always available increasing drug deaths of our citizens, and making healthcare harder for our seniors to get. We downplayed the family structure and led people to believe they were anything but what they really were or told them what they wanted to be had to be accepted in society. You know, transgender, homosexual, pedophile, and on and on. Marriage isn't necessary anymore, so just live together or live free and be whatever you want to be at any moment. Morally unacceptable and repulsive, but people bought into it even at the expense of our own children. We discouraged family life, and most one parent households are not able to encourage education and ethics. The kids who are lost make up the gangs, thieves, murderers and so on. All of the above contributes to our citizen base disappearing, and it is being replaced by unskilled and uneducated illegal immigrants.

It is easy then for politicians to control that type of person because the illegals often don't understand the country we had. Instead of people having choices and working to achieve their dreams, they take housing, food, healthcare, child care, and whatever else the government will give them and do as they are told. Many of them don't work at all, at least right now that is the way of it."

"What do you mean 'at least right now'?" Phil questioned.

Phineous started coughing, so his assistant brought him a glass of water. After his spell had passed, he ignored the reporter's question and looked out of the window as if searching for the next historical activity. He turned back to his guest, "And those abortions that government told all of the people they had a right to and should have. Do you know that over the years suicides for women who aborted a child have risen to twenty-five percent? I'll bet you didn't know that government started telling healthcare providers to give the woman aborting her child a deadly drug if she had any type of health or mental issue. Deaths for women during an abortion have risen twenty-seven percent in the last few years. These were women who could have lived many more years when they went in to receive 'care'. That way we eliminated unwanted citizens."

Phil was stunned. He stopped writing and could only stare at the person telling this grueling tale.

"That's right. And, if some women came back multiple times for abortions, they were given a drug that dried up their reproductive organs so they would be unable to conceive in the future. By telling people they were not accountable for their actions and they deserved to do what they wanted because morality was really a nonsensical concept, abortion was accepted and their conscience could justify killing an unborn child whenever they got themselves into trouble. That put their lives and future in the hands of government.

Phineous started coughing again but regained his voice quickly. "And, most of our people who wanted to go to college or change their lives had opportunities. They could have worked their way into their dream or gotten a grant or scholarship, but too many listened to the politicians and accepted what they were told about having no chance because of their race or income level.

And the magic solution was to depend on the government because 'they care about you'.

Because many believed some races were discriminated against, I among others thought it was the right time to stop whites from marrying whites. You know, stop white supremacy. We did that a year ago by making a law that no one could get married unless it's approved by a hack in the Administration, and that person won't approve a marriage between a white woman and white man unless of course it is a high-level politician or someone very rich. We repeated the words white supremacy so many times that people started believing and thought the marriage law was needed. Ridiculous!!!"

"So the idea was to make some people bad, and that worked to allow the government process of keeping people down or getting rid of almost an entire race in our country," Phil got angrier the more he spoke.

"That was part of it," Phineous answered. "Laws were made to make the people do as they were told while politicians became the masters. Some of the laws I and other congresspeople with an agenda helped get through kept people riled up over race, religion, security, and so on over the years. Look at the laws passed either through federal or state governments. Abortion, assisted suicide, gay rights, etc. that have diminished religious morals and allowed evil to invade society. Observe the world around you. Anything goes today even abusing our kids in the name of rights and feeling like part of the community. Feel good about yourself while you're sexually abusing a child or killing someone. The message is 'you belong'. A nation cannot survive by pushing God out and living on evil. People have lost their morality and for what? Are they happy now? But we confused the people so much, it kept the focus off of us and the blame on them. We did what we wanted while publicly focusing the people on illogical and detrimental behavior to confuse the masses so we could control the changes we wanted through laws we made or encouraged."

Phineous stopped again looking back over the years. The assistant approached the retired Congressman and stood by his side. "Yes, you are right," Handler looked at his aide and then at Phil. "I'm really too tired to go on today. Could you please come back perhaps Thursday afternoon, and we can continue?"

"Thursday will be fine," Phil smiled at the old man who was almost asleep in his chair. The reporter sat and watched the assistant push Handler out of the room. Picking up the recorder, he put it in his pocket and walked to the front door wondering how he could use the information he had just collected with all of the oppression in the current world everyone lived in.

CHAPTER TWO

Phil got home and listened to the conversation he'd recorded. He normally took lots of notes, but his pad had very little writing on it because he was too stunned at what he had heard Handler say. It was amazing that any politician would admit the things the old man confessed even though Phil knew they must be true. Was it possible that Phineous thought he could confess and when he died go to Heaven? The reporter didn't think any length of Purgatory could wash away what he had done cleansing him enough for an eternity with God. Of course, that was up to God alone.

Phil understood what he meant about the New Deal increasing the size of government and agreed with that being a good starting point in the country's demise. Certainly, government had grown over the years to put a strangle hold on the people.

"What other questions could I ask to get him to confess even more so we have all the pieces to the puzzle?" Phil wondered. "That probably isn't even feasible with the large number of politicians who worked to undermine our wonderful country. The old man probably wouldn't know all of what transpired to get to where our corrupt government had taken us."

Phil couldn't sleep that night, so he tried to read a book. That only worked for a little while. Television offered only propaganda and nothing he wanted to watch. Morning was coming soon, so he would see Bob and go from there.

The sunrise that morning was beautiful. He marveled at how something that picturesque could still exist in a world that had been ravaged and its people left destitute, sick, and helpless.

"Well," he thought, "God is still with us even though we are going through a time of transition. All of us turned a blind eye to at least some of what was going on. We didn't know everything, but none of us tried to find out either. We let filthy politicians turn our country into their empire leaving the people to serve them. Not once did the people mass together to let those in D.C. know they were done breaking our laws, done watching other politicians break laws, and lying to us. Now, only God could help get us out of this. We got what we deserved, so we either turn our lives around or live with this tyranny."

Every time Phil thought of all he had been told, he felt sick. "Okay, I've got to get past this and figure out how we can accomplish change." The sun shining through his window told him the office was open, so he went into the newspaper's headquarters and right to Bob's office. "Good morning, Bob. I got through my first meeting with Handler. I'd like you to hear what he said."

"Close the door and turn it on," his old friend told him.

"You aren't going to believe this," Phil said as he got the recorder out of his backpack and pushed play. The two men sat and listened.

"That was astonishing," Bob told his colleague. "I've never heard a politician talk like that. It's as if he knows he is going to die soon and recently discovered that sin really does exist."

"Yeah," Phil said sitting back in his chair, "but how are we going to get this out to the public without going to jail. You know they throw anyone in jail who speaks out against the regime."

"Yeah, I know," Bob said thinking about paths they could take. "Listen, I know a guy who was a special operations expert, and he hates what has happened to the country he defended and saw so many of his buddies die defending. Maybe we should talk to him and see if he has any suggestions."

"If you trust him, I guess I do to," his friend smiled. "Do you think we could meet with him tonight sometime? I have to go back to Handler's tomorrow."

"I'll give him a call and see. Sit right there." Bob picked up his phone and dialed.

"Hello," Gregg answered.

"Hey, Gregg, it's Bob. How you doing?"

"Long time buddy. I'm doing alright."

"What have you been up to?" Bob asked. "I haven't seen you at any of the political meetings."

"Well since I retired from the Marines, I've been trying to help other vets who are having problems. There are so many of them it's almost impossible. Our government forgot about those who served our late, great nation a long time ago, and now it seems they hate the civilians too. Anything big going on with the meetings? Any changes that are making a difference?" Gregg asked.

Bob looked over at Phil and then answered Gregg, "Nothing in the meetings. You know we get together quietly so we don't get into trouble with big brother watching every minute, and not everybody shows every week. That makes it tough to change anything."

Gregg sighed, "Yeah, that seems to be the way everything is going. We are so controlled, it's hard to get a handle on what we can do. The people in the Services certainly aren't allowed to honor the oath they took to defend the Constitution anymore."

Bob kind of chuckled, "That's the reason I called you buddy. Most of us want to change things but don't quite know how to do that. I have a reporter who just had a meeting with Phineous Handler. The old man confessed to multiple things, and he was recorded."

"Congressman Handler?" Gregg repeated. "Hell, I thought he died by now. What is he doing talking to a reporter?"

"Seems he believes he's dying soon and wants to confess," Bob answered. "We'd like you to come over to my office and listen to this recording and see if you can help us plan out a strategy to begin the contemporary reformation that is surely coming."

Gregg laughed, "I'd love to. When do you want me to come over?"

"How about tonight around six," Bob responded.

"Great, see you then," Gregg hung up wondering what he got Handler to say.

Phil looked at his boss, "What exactly can Gregg help us with?"

"He not only ran special ops, but he worked very closely with many at the Pentagon and with congressional politicians in D.C. He was a very respected part of government for many years. I think his wife still works for the Speaker of the House too."

That evening, Phil was in Bob's office when Gregg showed up. They listened to the recording and Gregg was amazed. "Are you going to meet with the old man again?"

"Yeah," Phil answered. "He said we could keep meeting as long as we need to so he can tell me everything he wants to get off his chest. He gets tired after about an hour or so and takes some kind of medication, but that only keeps him going a little while longer. Do you think we can use this stuff to turn our country back around?"

"Maybe," Gregg kept looking at the recorder. "We need to find out what the current and future plans are of these tyrants. What are they going to do next? You know, there are pockets of people across the country who are not abiding by this regime's orders. They govern themselves, marry who they please, grow their own crops, won't let illegals in, and they will not give up their guns when the government makes that a law. They are guarding their towns and not allowing the military anywhere near them. The inhabitants do everything for themselves. There is no way they will be dependent on these traitors. In fact, a group of us work with them to ensure there is communication between the sites that are on their own. Hopefully these areas will grow, because right now the government is still afraid of the people. But I'm afraid that the regime is planning something against these strongholds."

Bob asked, "Does your wife still work for the Speaker? How do you help them communicate and not put your wife in jeopardy?"

"My sister-in-law works for the Speaker. My wife works for the Chief of Staff at the White House, and yes, I suppose that may put her in danger if I were caught. The important thing is the two of them keep me informed on lots of issues, but the backroom meeting topics and decisions aren't let out to anyone," Gregg told them with seriousness. "That's why I don't know what they're working on or how bad it is. It will be very dangerous to work up a plan against what we are all facing."

Gregg paused for a minute and then looked at Phil, "You need to get him to tell you what the current and future plans are. He may not know, but I doubt that. They got him to retire but still value his advice on many subjects. Even if he acts stupid push to try and get what he knows."

"I will, but I have to let him talk and tell me what he wants to get off his mind. When I have a chance, I'll ask if he knows what the regime is planning to do next," Phil sounded doubtful, but the other two knew he would give it his best shot.

Thursday the reporter went back to Handler's and was escorted into the library. Phineous looked rested and happy. "Thank you for coming back," he told his guest.

Phil set the recorder on the table again and sat back waiting for the old Congressman to begin. Mentally, the reporter was hoping that an opportunity would come up for him to ask about politicians' plans being worked on in D.C.

"I know I gave you quite a bit to think about last time you were here," Phineous began, "but I have plenty more to tell you." He hesitated a minute looking at the reporter wondering what he was really thinking about all that had been told to him so far. "The next topic I want to tell you about is when I began to make more friends in foreign countries, and as our relationships grew, it was brought to my attention how beneficial it would be for both sides if I assisted in getting them our technical data and defense information, introduced bills that supplied foreign countries with money for research or funds to assist their countries, and offered any other type of assistance that would benefit them. Like many others in government, I didn't feel like the things I did could hurt our nation that much. By the time all of our shady deals were considered, we were causing devastating harm to our nation."

"But, of course, that didn't stop any of you from continuing to sell out our country?" Phil said sarcastically.

Handler breathed heavily. "No, actually our foreign contacts showed us how lucrative it would be to push for laws that increased taxes on domestic businesses. The laws passed hurt our industries enough to make many of them move to foreign countries where their profit margins were bigger. My foreign friends' income increased tremendously by businesses moving there. But of course, I didn't acknowledge the fact that our citizens were having trouble finding good paying jobs. But they were, because many of the higher paying companies moved overseas. Not my problem at the time."

Handler stopped to click his tongue and shake his head. "And the money that we voted in to send to foreign countries. Most of that money was laundered through a foreign business, lab, or some such entity and ninety percent was shared between us and the foreign government. The target for the money got about ten percent, and we stuffed our share in our bank accounts. American taxpayer dollars helped to make me and many others very rich."

19

"So," Phil added, "slowly some politicians ensured the United States became weaker while the foreign entities that made many of our politicians rich realized exponential growth and income. You all thought it was an accomplishment to use United States citizens' tax dollars for your own benefit and that of foreign adversaries. Right?"

Phineous nodded. Phil just watched the old man without a word, and Handler eyed the reporter as he took another drink.

The ex-Congressman began again, "You are looking at me as if I am a monster. Maybe you're right, maybe not. Things always depend on how you look at them. Was it wrong for people to be told by many in government that it was alright to riot, loot, and kill for reparations and justice? Was it wrong for many of us to tell people guns shoot people not people use guns to shoot people or make parents believe everything was alright in their schools and it was the pencils that failed tests when teachers didn't do their job? Because people do believe that it is always someone or something else's fault, it's easy to create chaos and confuse people so much that they believe anything you tell them. The public doesn't care what we're doing in D.C. or what the real cause of their problems of feeding and protecting their families or paying their bills are. They just listen to us tell them what's wrong and that it's someone else's fault."

"So you are justifying chaos and saying that what government told the public was right to keep focus off of what was being done behind citizens' backs?" Phil looked as if the retired Congressman was being ridiculous.

"Yes," Phineous said. "Sometimes and for some people that way is more beneficial for them. If the government takes care of everything, they don't worry about it or justify actions. They take what is given to them and live their lives the best they can."

Phil didn't buy what Handler said. "You and others may see yourselves as saviors and rulers of the people, but all of our citizens don't accept that."

"I agree, but the facts show for themselves. Sixty percent of our citizens depend on government for everything and don't question what we do. That's a huge percentage that the government takes care of. When a senior gets ill, they now go to a government directed doctor and believe they're

20

getting excellent care. What they aren't told is that medical attention today is based on age and physical ability, so many of them out there will not get the care they need. Too expensive for the Administration. Good care is for younger able-bodied people, the rich, and political families. The medical care and medicine given to seniors and those with disabilities won't help them, but they believe it will. Eventually with the poor care they get, they will die."

"How do any of you live with yourselves? I would think every one of you would be scared to death to die after what you've done to other human beings." Phil was astonished.

"Most of us have no problem living or lose no sleep. But people don't understand the medical care available and that it is planned to quicken death for the older and sickly ones."

The two looked at each other as if they were having a duel, and the reporter did not look away first.

"And then there's the peoples' money and assets we wanted to dip into. Towards the end of my service, the new technology that renewed itself almost daily allowed us to look into everything people owned or were buying. From there, we could take funds claiming they were making too much money or had too many assets and had to pay more taxes. The taxes were for regular citizens, but not politicians or the rich. That was the real beginning of the redistribution you've heard about. People used to think redistribution of wealth was to take someone's money and give it to another who didn't have as much. Citizens didn't perceive that the government could redistribute money and property to itself and give out what it wanted to each person. So as this concept develops, the ones who had little and thought they would get much from others will still have nothing."

Phineous took a little break and had some tea and crackers. His guest declined the refreshments. After a few minutes, the old man started again, "Of course, there still isn't a budget. Congress stopped passing budgets long ago. The politicians keep printing money to lavish on foolish projects and to pay for necessities for our citizens who don't or can't work and seventy percent of the people who are not citizens but have thronged into our country illegally. As the money becomes worth less and less, it costs more and more to buy food or pay bills. This again pushes more people on assistance and gives the

Administration that much more power. The government allowed those who wanted to be taken care of to realize that. You know, a democracy is of the people, by the people, and for the people. But democracy and freedom end when most people depend on the government, and the ability of the Administration to take care of people slowly ends when too many depend on it. We are getting to the point where there will be no funds to take care of those who can't or won't work. It took years for the legislators who wanted power to turn the tables, but as you can see the different branches of government have proclaimed themselves rulers and no longer public servants. And they can do that because they won't be challenged."

Again, the old man stopped and was breathing a little hard. He rested for a minute and drank some more water. Phil was starting to feel uncomfortable and stood, but Phineous waved his hand for the reporter to sit back down.

Phil was still offended by what the old man had said and told the retired Congressman, "Now most people who depend on the government for sustenance don't get enough food, and their living conditions are terrible."

"That support is what more than half of our people asked for," Handler continued his argument, "and with the burden of the illegal immigrants, there isn't enough to go around for everyone. Those communities that still fend for themselves have a much nicer life."

"Wasn't it the government who let all those illegals flow in? Now you are telling me that our people going hungry and living in rat traps for the most part is their fault. That is really rich!" the reporter did not believe the argument set before him. He rose to leave.

"I'm not finished for today yet, so please sit down. As you know, we have Chinese and other foreign military on our soil. We sold so much of our land and so many buildings and homes to foreigners, they want to be able to protect their interests. I had petitioned for years to cut the military budget, and that is what we did. Now, half of the military on our land is foreign. They aren't here to protect us I can assure you, but they are here to learn all about our technology and processes. They are hoping one day soon to walk up to a microphone and tell our people they are now citizens of another country. Pretty bad huh?"

"I thought their militaries were only here for training purposes as allies," Phil looked startled. "Our Administration is alright with this?"

"Most everyone thinks foreign military is training here, but unfortunately, that is not the case. Now our military is dwindling while the communist military on our land is growing. The draft was taken away many years ago, so half the military that we have left only care about a paycheck, college education, and maybe a sex change. The other half of our military is powerless and can't keep the oath they took. So combined, they have to protect the traitors and the criminals in our government. Most of our Administration is fine with all of that," the retired Congressman shook his head. "And our government is absolutely alright with the communist foreign regimes. The top layer of American government and the rich believe their taking over will allow them to be the emperors here while all the people become slaves like the foreign countries. Government does everything they can to achieve this.

Many of our businesses have moved away, so for decades we buy most everything from other countries and especially from the communist ones. Then what did our esteemed leaders do? They took the tariffs off what these same communist countries import in to us. We pay for the non-tariff trade they are doing in our country because our people pay plenty to sell any of our products in their countries.

Then, we have let them ship in all the drugs they want and have done that for years. They sell and our people have died in the millions over the last decades because of this. The communists are making trillions of dollars, so that means our people are paying for the land, technology, and buildings communists buy in our country from their drug trade. They can also afford the land in other countries to strategically take over the world."

Phil couldn't believe such traitors were in our midst and getting rich by selling our nation out. It was almost too much to take in.

"Let me continue," Phineous said. "As I stated before, what really helped all of the goals I and others had was the new technology that everyone bought into. A lot of that is from communist countries too. Fun stuff, and everyone can obtain information quickly. Of course, now officials can watch anyone and track what they do. The facts can be skewed or created with the right programs, and that means they can pick their targets and cause anyone to

23

be charged with anything. It was just a matter of talking people into how wonderful and useful new technology is. Many people still don't realize the harm instant communication and surveillance can do, so they readily go along with it. The media is too stupid to put two and two together and goes along with supporting the tech giants."

Phineous started to cough, and his assistant rushed over with a glass of water. It took him a few minutes, and then he was finally ready to go on.

"Not only that, but for the last decade or so our government has taken our energy away leaving us dependent on communist countries to supply the green energy equipment that just had to be used here in the States. The communist countries thrive on fossil fuels, and the weather or heat index of the earth hasn't changed a bit after trillions of dollars were put into clean energy that doesn't produce enough to take care of our folks. I helped to get that done too. Now, many of our people freeze in the winter and die of the heat in the summer."

Phil looked at Handler without flinching. "Yes, technology allows all of the things you talked about, but technology doesn't have to be used that way. I hope all those who are pushing our country into a communist state suffer terribly on this earth and in the next life. All who participate hate our country, but why? Our nation was the greatest that had ever been with opportunity for those who chose to achieve."

"I don't hate our country, but you are right, some do. It all comes down to power, and I was one who wanted that power. Why do you think English was never made our official language? Oh sure, some states dubbed it their official language, but their laws carry no clout. I was one who wanted people from all over the world to stream in here. I now call us the 'Land of Babble'. We can't even talk to each other, and there are too many different cultures to count. People lived around cities by others who spoke their language and shared their beliefs. Workers were used who could communicate with those they served. So what did politicians come up with? They ensured people who could understand each other had to live in the same area of the city. That is segregation to the fullest. To top that off, these people have no idea of what is going on in other cities because they get propaganda for their immediate area in their language. The color of their skin isn't important anymore, but the language they speak is and is used to separate the masses. Most of the people who flooded our country have no skills and no choice to live where they want. They are managed by the Administration and work for the privileged or the cruel drug cartels."

Phil couldn't believe what Handler was confessing. "It seems to me we have the devil and his fiends running our government. Please don't forget Congressman, the devil can be taken down. God has the power to do that, so I wouldn't be too cocky if I were you or any politician who worked for this."

The two stared at each other. Phil suddenly realized something, "It was you and people like you who made many feel hopeless and stripped of any say they would have. Suicides have been much higher for people who are in despair. Higher than even the drug related deaths caused by the cartels bringing in lethal drugs. Of course, these things aren't reported except for a few honest stations that are being ridiculed and treated viciously. People can be replaced, but power, land, riches, those things are limited, isn't that right? For a great deal of the politicians their motto is 'it's us first, America never'."

Phineous wasn't even trying to smile anymore. He continued with what he wanted to say. "The final blow that will take every bit of hope away from the people will come when government takes all guns away from them. Many, many have already surrendered and have given up their arms. Some wanted mental health care improved to stop shootings. Well, that isn't going to happen nationwide. The people will follow the uncaring leadership and will allow all guns to be taken for good very soon. That will leave our people without any way to protect themselves, and that is when they become true slaves. When that happens, the politicians will not be afraid of the people anymore. The officials and the rich will be guarded by security with guns. Do you think those on top will ever let go of the hold they have on the populace once that happens? Hell no!"

Handler started to chuckle, "The really funny thing though is that most everyone I worked with from this country and bought off or sold favors to will fall to the bottom of the pit once the takeover is complete. They will become nobodies just like the citizens they lied to, hurt, and caused nothing but heartache to. Those so happy to be courted by the powers running the government accomplished whatever was asked of them and will slowly lose their money and their way of living. None of them will mean anything to those who end up on top. I don't imagine they will get too much sympathy from true citizens, so I guess that will be some type of reparation."

He looked at Phil very seriously, "They threw me out of 'the club' because they thought I was getting too old and was growing a conscience. I understood this because I killed many careers and people too by taking away what they had and ruining their lives anyway I could. Lying, cheating, etc. When they sold me down the river, I knew what to expect. I was old enough and smart enough to keep my money, and I have lived well since our country started to die. It's a dirty game, but that's the way it works.

Now, I look over the life I was given and see how poorly I used it. In fact, I have to laugh at myself for putting so much emphasis on my career and the wealth and power I could obtain without considering I cannot take any of that with me. The money, power, and status will mean nothing when I leave this earth, and I know my day of judgement is right around the corner. For the past few years, I have regretted my actions more each day. Remembering those who worked beside me with constant faith in God and truly serving the people weighs on my conscience. I ask for forgiveness, but it is up to the Lord whether He will grant that or not. The same with our citizens. They will forgive or they will not."

Phil sat there not knowing what to say. The confession he had just received was definitely from a man who could not live with himself any longer. Everyone who could think logically knew the government had caused the country to fail, but he never expected to hear such a graphic version of Handler's part of the destruction. "Have you tried to repair any of the damage that you caused? I mean for people you hurt or to try and turn our country around?"

Phineous looked Phil squarely in the eye, "No, I can't say that I have. What you see," Handler motioned around them, "is what I worked for during my government service, and most of my actions to achieve what I wanted were worked behind the scenes the entire time I was pretending to serve. I was good at telling constituents everything was for their own good. It is sad to see what I have done and helped others to do. Government is slowly taking over everything, and all of the things I spoke of will culminate in the United States becoming a third world country."

Phil could see the old man was angry at himself. But the reporter felt no sympathy for someone so careless with others' lives.

"So what are they planning now?" Phil looked at the old man hoping he was mad enough to tell him something they could use to take a stand against the regime.

"I don't know if they have any plans except to keep a strangle hold on the people. What else do they need?" Handler shrugged.

"Well, there are still regions and small towns that haven't succumbed to anything the government has been doing or pushing on people. So what about those places?" Phil pressed on.

"The only reason those areas exist is because the time has not come yet for the Administration to take complete control. I believe the current President is too weak and does not have the courage to fire on the places that refuse to give up their independence. The government is still afraid that shooting at its own people will cause a revolt. But sooner or later something will happen to capture those who are rebelling against the status quo."

"How come more towns didn't defy the lunacy?" Phil asked.

"Because the larger cities can't or won't figure out a way to fend for themselves. They have been used to a great deal of government assistance and local politicians telling the people what to do while believing higher level officials were 'handling' things for citizens. Many smaller communities can fend for themselves, and more and more will take that route until the government can figure out how to stop them."

"You think the government will harm the communities that continue to refuse to be manhandled by them?" the reporter looked at the old man with disbelief.

Handler shook his head as if Phil hadn't been listening, "Of course they will, and whatever path they choose to take they will get away with it. What astounds me is that not one of the people in charge who continued down the path of destruction against the peoples' will was ever held accountable. We used our positions to harass and hurt those who disagreed with us, we took the peoples' tax money and used it foolishly, many took money from foreign entities, sold out our country, and are making laws to take away the peoples' rights. But not one of these officials has received or is receiving any punishment! If justice had been demanded and officials knew they would be prosecuted or shamed and the result would be imprisonment for treason, the posture of our country would never be where it is now. But we all reassured our constituents everything was alright and threw them a couple of bones to get voted back in."

Phil had had enough, "And still, you do nothing to assist your country."

Phineous looked at Phil and then looked away. The reporter felt like Handler knew something but wasn't telling.

"I think that is enough for today," the old man said. "I'm very tired."

"Do you need me to come back?" Phil asked. "It sounds like we are at the end of your story."

Handler was certain he was working with a very shrewd person, and he knew he had to tell the reporter the rest of what was going to happen if he had a chance at spending eternity where he wanted. "I'll call you if I want to meet again. We may have more to discuss, but I need to go over my daily journal to see if there is anything else that needs to be told."

Phil agreed and knew he was right that Handler was holding back. Why he would do that, the reporter couldn't tell. "Let me know, and I'll be glad to come back if that is what you want."

He stood up and bent down to shake Handler's hand. Picking up his recorder and sliding it into his pocket, he turned and walked to the door of the library. Phil stopped suddenly and turned back to his host, "Do you have contact with the Pentagon much anymore or any of the Services?"

"No," Phineous looked confused. "Why would I?"

"Just wondered," the reporter smiled. "I know you used to deal with both quite a bit and wondered if you still had contacts there."

Handler just shook his head, and the reporter left the room.

CHAPTER THREE

Friday, Phil and Bob were talking in Bob's office when Gregg and several of his friends walked in.

"Hi guys," Gregg smiled. "This is Mark, Max, Leo, and Gunman, Marines I used to serve with."

Phil flipped his hand up to say hi, and Bob smiled at the group. The reporter got out the recorder, "Here's what I got yesterday from Handler." He sat the recorder on the table, and the men took seats to listen to what Handler had to say.

When the recording had finished, Phil shut it off and looked at the others. Leo channeled his frustration right away, "They've been planning to take all guns for a long time. The politicians have harped about guns for so long that seventy percent have turned in their arms I heard. They think the killing will stop, but it won't."

Max rubbed his chin and looked at Gregg, "There's a lot of dirt there, but who would we take it to? The government would throw us in jail, and too many citizens would tell on us hoping to increase their popularity with those in power."

Gregg thought for a minute and then looking at Phil asked, "Are you going back to Handler's?"

"Only if he calls me back. Right now I'm just on stand-by."

Gregg looked concerned, "He knows what they're planning, and if he calls you back, you have to find out what that is. I'm sure it will be something against the communities that are not doing things the government's way."

"I think he knows too," Phil responded. "His body language and facial expression told me the same thing."

"Let me take this recorder, and I'll try to come up with a plan," Gregg said almost talking to himself. Then he turned back to Phil, "Do you have another one in case Phineous calls you back?"

"Yeah, I've got another," the reporter smiled at his new friend.

The group said goodbye, and Phil headed for home. He didn't have to work the next day, so he was thinking about going to visit his parents who lived about ten miles away. He procrastinated about the journey and ended up not calling his parents to tell them he would be there. "If I still want to go in the morning, I'll call them then," he told himself as he crawled into bed.

About midnight Phil's phone started ringing. He jumped out of bed afraid that something terrible had happened to someone in his family. "Hello!"

"This is Congressman Handler's assistant," the voice sounded quiet and urgent. "The Congressman would like you to come over right away."

Phil looked at the clock. "It's midnight. Couldn't this wait until tomorrow?"

"No," the assistant answered. "The Congressman's health has taken a turn for the worse, and he would like to talk to you as soon as possible."

"I'll be there as quickly as I can," Phil was startled by the news.

He dressed hastily, and as he started out the door he stopped suddenly. Rummaging in a drawer he found a recorder he could take. Once he was out into the night, he became very aware of the silence all around. Not even a dog barked, and there was no wind to rustle the leaves. Finally getting to Handler's house, he walked up to the door and knocked. The assistant answered almost immediately.

"Please come in, sir." The guest followed the aide up several flights of stairs and into the bed chamber of Phineous Handler.

The assistant bent down close to Handler's ear and whispered that his visitor had arrived. He motioned for Phil to take a seat next to the bed so he could converse with the old man more easily. Removing the recorder from his pocket, Phil turned it on and held it in his hand hoping to capture information that would help his group come up with a plan.

Handler looked white as if he were already a ghost, and his skin was sunken and slack. As the reporter looked around, he noticed the room was cold and damp. Only a few candles flickered in the background which made the furniture placed around the sides of the room look huge. Phil didn't see any paintings on the walls or personal articles lying on the tops of the tables or dressers. As he continued to scan the room, he noticed a small table in the corner with a picture of a lady setting on top. He had no idea if that was Handler's wife, mother, or perhaps another relative of long ago.

Very slowly Phineous spoke with a low, hoarse voice, "They are going to set bombs off in the independent areas that won't follow their laws."

Phil looked at the man as if he was crazy. "Are you saying that some politicians are going to order an attack on our own people on our land?"

Phineous nodded slightly. He drew a shallow breath and continued. "They're going to kill the President and take complete control of the entire government. Only chance to reverse this is for our people to turn back to God for assistance and then take a united stand against the politicians quickly." Handler started to gasp for air, and a doctor appeared next to the visitor.

"Do you know when this is going to happen?" Phil asked breathlessly.

"Please move away from the patient," the doctor told the reporter. Phil stood up and moved to the foot of the bed. The doctor turned up the oxygen that was flowing into the patient's nose. The gasping continued, so the doctor took out a syringe and gave the old man a shot. In the next couple of minutes, Congressman Phineous Handler was dead.

The doctor whispered to the assistant and left the room. Phil looked at the aide and followed the doctor out. Once outside the house, the reporter stood looking at the window in the upper floor wondering if Phineous was being judged by his Maker at that very moment or if he had already been judged and sent where he would spend eternity. "I wonder where the Lord is sending the old man. Had he done enough penance and given enough reparation? Wow, he almost sounded like he was having a vision as he spoke his last words."

It was two in the morning by the time Phil got home, and once inside his door he wondered what he was going to do? How could he let the people in those communities know what was going to happen to them? Then he remembered that Gregg had contacts there and could warn them. "Bob should be up by seven," he thought, "so I'll be at his house then. He can contact Gregg and let him know what's going on."

Phil was sitting on the first step of Bob's house when his boss got out of bed and went to the front door to get the newspaper. He saw his reporter and told him to come inside. "What are you doing out there?" he was amused.

"You're not going to think this is so funny once you hear what I've got," the reporter told his boss. "You better get Gregg on the line."

Bob was perplexed but called Gregg. "Hi Gregg, this is Bob. Phil is at my house, and he has something for us to hear."

31

"Okay," Gregg waited patiently.

Phil looked at Bob and then began, "I was called to Handler's last night because the old man took a turn for the worse. Here is what he said." He played the recording for the two, and when it was over there was complete silence.

Finally, Gregg spoke up, "Was he serious? Did he say when this was going to happen? We have to have more."

"Sorry pal," the reporter answered, "Handler died when I was in the room."

"Shit," Gregg said. "I can contact the communities and tell them about the bombs, but we can't tell them who to look for. This will scare them all to death, and we don't know if it's going to be tomorrow or in a month. I'll get ahold of the ones I know and put them on alert, but this is going to be messy. I'll have to let my wife know too."

"She can't tell anybody," Phil objected. "If the people on the Hill know we have this info, they'll come after us. And don't doubt that they'd kill us for the recorders and for even knowing this stuff. That means your wife too."

"Well, I have to let her know so she can keep an eye out for anything suspicious. I hope this is just an end of life joke on those he hated," Gregg couldn't believe what Phil uncovered.

Bob understood the way Gregg was feeling, "Look, tell your wife, but tell her to keep it to herself until we can find out more. That type of activity would take a lot of planning for so many locations, so hopefully we have some time."

Gregg agreed, and Phil did as well telling them he wouldn't do anything until they had come up with a way to handle this.

Across the city in an afterhours encounter at seven o'clock two days later, several senators and congressmen gathered secretly in a meeting room at the Capitol. The voices of the attendees rose and fell as they discussed the plan they were putting into place.

"Look," Jacob Peterson, Speaker of the House, said, "we've taken years to get into the position we are in, and with all of the spending that Congress has passed over the last decade and all the spending the President has done with Executive Orders, our country is finally on the verge of economic collapse. Our debt has been so high, we are paying huge interest rates to borrow more. Now, the total interest on the payments we make is way more than the money we have to pay it back, so of course we've been printing lots more money. For the last month, we have seen inflation mushroom. We have come to the point that the government will not be able to sustain the spending that is going on, and Social Security, Medicare, Medicaid, rent assistance, food assistance, and so on are not going to be able to continue to be paid. In the next few months all of the assistance to the seniors and the lower income people will have to stop, and when that happens there is going to be rioting in the streets. This President knows this but is just dragging his feet. Instead of working with us for the complete government takeover of everything, he just tells us to back off a bit. He's not going to push anything. Elections are coming up in less than a year, and if the majority changes in the House or Senate, it could be years before we get to our final destruction of this damn democracy. Hey, we all believe that a communist third world country is the way to go, so we have to take action and get rid of this President. Our plan will take the peoples' focus off what we've done to them over the last decade, and it will put their direct focus on surviving in a world turned upside down. Most people will do what we say because of the circumstances they find themselves in."

Senator Lucy Katrin looked at Jacob, "You're right. We've done alright so far, but we have to get past this last hump and begin the final power lock in. I know this has taken years, but it takes time to gain the trust of the people before taking action against them. We'll take it step by step and think things through carefully. Look how much we have gained, and more than half of the people still believe what we tell them. They are all turning their weapons in now except the holdout areas. We'll follow our plan and destroy the independent communities that won't give up their guns and a few other towns so the bombings won't look like they were for targeted areas. Once we destroy those places and have all of their firearms, we'll put everyone who was against us in one of the rebel camps we're setting up. When we do that, we can finish implementing our plan and have total power. Working with the foreign governments will give us resources we don't have now, and so it won't matter

33

how many of our people die or are destitute. We'll be rich and so will all of the powerful people who have been backing us. Forming bonds with the foreign governments has enabled us to increase our power, and as soon as our plan is put into action, our power will spread around the world. Jacob, did we get the money back from the Chinese projects?"

"We did," Jacob smiled. "They laundered the money through one of their tech companies. The four of us got thirty-five percent, China got forty-five percent, and twenty percent went to the projects. Wish our government wasn't so broke. We could take kickbacks like this more often by passing bills to give them more funds for 'projects'. Well anyway, thank you American taxpayers for all of the perks you give us."

The others laughed and resumed reviewing the plan they had been devising for months. All of the members at the meeting had served in Congress for at least twenty years, and they were tired of being called public servants.

Senator Justin Pebbles threw his pencil on the table and looked at the Speaker, "And by the way, Jacob, keep those piss ant newbies away from me. They think they are going to take over and save the world. Dumb shits walk in and after a year think they're going to tell us what to do. I don't think so!"

"They aren't going to accomplish anything," Jacob snapped. "We need them to vote yes on the things we want passed, and already a few of them are having second thoughts. Just smile and act interested, and when we get what we want, we'll dump them."

"To hell with them," Lucy spoke sharply. "We've got votes to pass what we want and then we'll get rid of all of them. We just won't need them anymore."

Jack Shiver, another congressman, glanced around the table at the others. "Look, I've got to go. Let's meet Thursday night same time and we'll finish this plan so we can move on. I'll see you then." He got up and walked to the door looking back at the group and shaking his head as if he must be crazy.

"Guess we might as well quit for the night. That bastard leaves early every meeting, so I wonder if he's really serious about this. We better keep an eye on him. We'll meet back here Thursday night, and it better be the last time," Jacob scowled.

In the Longworth Building Jacob's top aide, Jody, waited for him to return so she could leave. She was finished with her work and was bored, so she called her twin sister. "Hey Jamie, I'm still stuck at the office waiting for Peterson to get back. Should be out of here in the next half hour, so I'll meet you at the Knoll about eight-thirty."

"Okay," Jamie said, "we need to talk, so get a booth in the back."

They hung up, and Jody took some emails into Peterson's office and laid them on his desk. She saw an email that didn't come through her laying on top of his stack of projects. "What the hell! This is from Pebbles, and I thought Peterson hated him." She read the memo, "Meeting is on tonight. Getting closer to total power!" Jody heard people walking down the hall and hurried back to her desk. Sitting down quickly, she acted like she was working on her computer.

Jacob walked quickly through the door, "Thanks for staying, Jody. I'll be leaving in a little while, so go ahead and go home. See you tomorrow."

Jody smiled as he disappeared into his office. She picked up her things and walked down to the entrance of the building. Once outside she inhaled the fresh air in deeply. For some reason, the air was always refreshing once she left the large office building.

She took the subway across town and got off at Foggy Bottom. From there she walked the few blocks to the Knoll Bar. The place was packed and she looked around to see if her sister was there yet. Slowly, she navigated through the people finally getting to the back of the bar. She spotted one booth that was empty at the very end. The waitress was there immediately to get her order. "Sangria," Jody smiled. She got her phone out and started going through her messages getting lost in the gossip from her friends at work.

"Hi," Jamie said as she plunked down on the bench opposite her sister. "You certainly are involved with whatever you're doing there."

They both started laughing, and the waitress brought Jody's drink and took Jamie's order, "Draft beer, any kind."

"Listen," Jamie leaned in speaking in a low, serious tone. "There is something very strange going on. Lots of hush hush around the Big House. Today at a meeting with the other staffers, Tim said there's a group in Congress who are planning to get rid of the President and take power."

"That sounds pretty ridiculous, doesn't it?" Jody asked. "Although I did see an email today from Pebbles that talked about a meeting and total power."

"That's got to be the same thing," Jamie sat back quickly moving over to let her husband sit down. "Gregg, you were in special ops, and word is out that a power struggle is going on and the President is going to be the target."

Gregg looked at his wife and quietly talked to the ladies, "Do you remember Phineous Handler?" Both girls nodded. "He told a friend of mine that what you just said is going to happen. Those trying to steal power are also going to bomb the small communities that haven't followed everything the government has passed into law. This has to be kept very quiet. You can't leak this out to one person, because they will get rid of anyone who knows their plan."

"Are you sure Handler knew what he was talking about?" Jamie was skeptical.

Gregg smirked, "We'll find out. Handler died right after he told his story."

Just a few miles from the Knoll bar, Lucy knocked on the door of a Ritz-Carlton hotel room. Jacob Peterson opened the door wearing a smile and a bathrobe. She went in, and the door shut softly. He folded her into his arms and walked her over to the bed. He caressed her body and made her moan with delight as he made passionate love to her.

After a while, they laid in bed and she rubbed his chest softly as he kissed her forehead. "You're such a good lover," she told him. And after a few minutes, she whispered, "We're going to get caught if we keep this up."

"Who'd care?" he said sarcastically. "My wife is on a cruise and probably trying to pick up a man. Hell, she doesn't care if I don't go home at all unless she needs me to take her to a party."

They quit talking as they caressed each other and peered off into space thinking about their lives. Lucy looked up at him, "Do you really think we can pull this final power grab off? Lots can go wrong."

"Yeah, I think we'll do it," Jacob was totally relaxed. "Then no more public servants but leaders who will lead by back breaking laws.

Not far from the Ritz, another member of the conspiracy group was relaxing at the R & L Bar. Justin Pebbles took a drink and saw a friend walk in, Senator Vic Blacken. Vic saw him and sat down to chat as he ordered a drink.

"How's the plan coming? We almost there?" Vic smiled at his friend.

"Shit, I don't know how far we should push our ideas," Justin looked at his drinking companion. "Too much can go wrong."

Vic looked around the bar, "I'm glad you told me about the plan you four have. There won't be any problems. With Peterson in the lead, he'll know who to talk to. I'll do my part when that time comes around, but I wonder if he'll try to dump us once we vote everything he wants in."

Justin shrugged, "Do you think the right and left will come together on the laws we want to pass?"

Vic chuckled, "There isn't a right or left. All but a handful are after the same thing we are. They're tired of hearing from public idiots, and they intend to change everything even if it takes installing a caste system."

Justin looked shocked, "How in the hell would we make up a caste system and move people into it?"

Vic smiled with arrogance, "We just take everything they have away."

They both started to laugh and raised their glasses in a toast.

CHAPTER FOUR

In the dark of the night, an ex-FBI agent, Randy, worked with his friend, Tom, going over some maps of the United States. They were at Randy's house which was a small, musty smelling place. Randy had been forced to retire from the FBI because he didn't always believe in the way the FBI did things. The years he spent at the Agency taught him how laws could be avoided and actions taken without accountability. When he objected, he was ostracized, and they drove him into retirement. From that day on, he decided he didn't have to go by the law either.

"We need to get this finished," Randy looked at Tom. "They want these now."

"How much are you getting paid to do this?" his buddy asked him.

"Don't worry about what I'm getting. I'm paying you plenty, so shut up and help me get this done."

The two continued to circle small towns and communities on state maps. The targets were places the people paying them wanted taken care of. So far, they had thirty-seven maps done and were getting closer to completion of the entire list Peterson had given to Randy. The retired FBI agent had people lined up to detonate bombs at the locations they circled and felt exhilarated with the prospect of making a name for himself.

He hated politicians, but he knew that working with Peterson would give him the opportunity to strike back at the entire government he loathed. He especially wanted to hurt the executive branch which was his main target. Randy didn't care how Peterson got his name for the job, but he wanted to make certain he was kept undercover so as much damage as possible could be done.

The next day, Jody got to work a little early, and her boss was already in his office. She saw his personal line in use, and that confused her because she knew his wife and kids were not at home. He could use the line for anyone, but his strict rule was that the line was for his immediate family only in case there was ever an emergency. She decided to call her sister.

"Hi. Peterson is already in his office, and he's on his line that is for immediate family only. His family is on a cruise, so who's he talking to?"

"Well walk something into his office that will take you a few minutes to do and listen," Jamie almost whispered.

Jody grabbed some emails and knocked lightly on the door before opening it. Jacob looked up and stopped talking.

"What is it, Jody?"

"Just wanted to bring in some emails. A couple of them look important," she answered with a smile.

Peterson reached his hand out for them and then motioned her out of the room. She left but didn't close the door completely. After checking that the main entrance door was shut, she went back by Jacob's door to see if she could hear anything.

Jacob started talking again, "I told you I want those maps and the list by tomorrow." He slammed the phone down and picked it up right away. "Lucy, I'm coming to see you. Are you sure Randy is the guy we need? A guy named Tom is helping him, but they don't have the maps or list we need yet. I'm on my way."

Jody pulled his office door shut quietly and sat down quickly grabbing a piece of paper to read.

"I'm going to see Senator Katrin, and I'll probably be gone until after lunch." Jacob disappeared out the door as Jody smiled at him and then turned back to reading. She waited a minute and then went into his office to see if she could tell who he had been talking to on the first call and what it was about.

Looking around his desk and then around the fax machine, she saw nothing. Jody went back to his desk and took a closer look at some of the papers strewn across the top. Suddenly she remembered that he put things in his top right drawer that were important, so she slid the drawer open. Flipping through some papers, she found one that he had doodled on. The words written were BOMBS, RANDY, AND TERRORISTS. She hurried out of his office.

"Jamie, we need to talk," Jody was adamant as her sister answered the phone.

Jamie paused, "I'm pretty busy. Can't you tell me over the phone?"

"No!" her sister insisted. You know the phones around here have static sometimes so calls overlap!"

"Oh yes," Jamie understood, "Let's meet at noon outside your office by the wagons."

There were so many hungry people at the lunch wagons ready for a break at noon that Jamie and Jody bought lunch and moved away from the crowd. They sat by a relaxing water fountain, and Jamie breathed in the fresh air and closed her eyes as she tilted her head towards the sun.

"Look at this!" Jody put the paper she found in Jamie's hand. "I heard him talking, and he wants info by tomorrow from this jerk. Terrorists!!!!"

"You don't know anything yet," Jamie looked intently at her sister. "Calm down. I'll talk to Gregg and see what he says. He'll know what to do."

Jody agreed and they sat quietly and ate their lunch. Both were afraid they had stumbled onto something that would quickly blowup all around them. When lunch was finished, they gave each other a hug and then went back to their own offices.

Jacob never returned to his office that day, so Jody left at her normal time. She decided to stop by the market and then went home to cook dinner. Just as she sat down to eat, her telephone rang, so she looked to see who was calling.

"Hi Jamie, what did you find out?"

Jamie sighed, "I talked to Gregg. He took the paper, and he's going to talk to some of his buddies who are still in the Service to see if they've heard anything. I know he is really worried. Tomorrow, find out anything else you can."

Jody talked to her sister about what Gregg thought and then shut her phone off. She had a very bad feeling about this. How was she going to find out anything else unless she followed Peterson? Well, she'd do her best.

The next morning when Jody got to the office, Peterson was there before her again. As she walked to her desk, she could hear people talking in his office. She sat at her desk straining to hear what they were saying. In the next minute a strange man walked out of Jacob's office leaving the door open and went out the front door without saying a word to her.

Jacob was still in his office looking over the list he was just given. She heard him pick up the phone and call Lucy. "Hey Lucy, meeting is on tonight. I just got everything we need. Tell the others."

Jody poked her head into his office, "I've got to run an errand."

He waved her off, and she grabbed her phone on the way out. Hurrying down to the entrance of the Longworth Building she stepped outside scanning the people for the man who just left. She found him and waited until he turned his head her way. When she saw his face, she snapped a picture of him. The picture was sent to Jamie's phone, and then she showed the guard her badge to get back into the building. She sat down at her desk wondering what that man had to do with all of this.

That night in a dimly lit meeting room, the four conspirators met again. Jacob laid the maps and a list on the table. "These maps show the areas that will be hit tomorrow. And here is the list of people who will ensure what we want done is accomplished."

Lucy looked at the maps, "Do we really want to hurt our own people?"

Jacob smiled at her, "Most of the sites chose their own path and destiny. None of them would listen to reason which I call insurrection. We'll take all of their guns and move them to other areas. The other neutral places we wanted were added in, and that should clear us of everything."

"Who picked the people who will do it?" Jack asked.

"Don't worry about that," Jacob responded. "It's done, and that's what we need."

Justin looked around the table. "Okay, what happens after the dirty bombs are set off?"

"They aren't really dirty bombs," Jacob told them. "We are just going to tell the people radioactive material was propelled into the air by the bombs so we can herd those areas holding out into towns we already run. We don't want to ruin our land and put ourselves in danger. Those setting off the bombs think they are radioactive as well, so we have all the bases covered and no one will know. Of course, the sites will be guarded by our military, so all we have to do is say the radioactivity readings were very bad and no one will know the difference."

Lucy smiled at Jacob, "And after it's done, we take over. We know where the President and Vice President will be tomorrow, and they will be made powerless. We have a person in the Pentagon at a high level who will make certain the military is at our disposal."

"Who takes control; who speaks to the public?" Jack asked.

"I'm the Speaker of the House," Jacob snapped. "I'll do that, and the rest of you can stand around me."

Justin looked skeptical, "Do you think the public will buy this?"

Lucy laughed, "Over fifty percent of citizens believe anything we tell them. And of course, we have eighty-five percent of the media reporting what we tell them."

"Then we move the people who survived the bombings out and tell the public how we are handling everything." Justin sat back in his chair.

Jacob chuckled, "That's right. As soon as possible, we'll finish making the laws we want and they will be irreversible."

"This is big!" Lucy smirked. "After tomorrow, we will never go back to what our country used to be."

Each picked up a map and started looking over the towns that were circled. Jacob took the list of people who would place and detonate the bombs and put it in his jacket pocket. Those were names he didn't need to share with the others.

The next morning, Jacob's group huddled in his office with the TV on. None of them spoke, but they all concentrated on the news wondering how long it would be before any type of news flash was reported.

The TV host they had been watching suddenly stopped the interview he was doing and told the audience that a breaking story had just come in. "We have just gotten a special report. Bombs have been detonated in many areas across the United States. No one knows the number yet, but the reports indicate that a large number of people have been killed and injured. Radioactive material has been released from all of the explosions. People need to stay indoors until officials determine how harmful the radioactive material is and what actions should be taken. We'll bring you more updates as they come in."

Right then, Jody got an alert from Capitol Hill security on her computer. The four in Jacob's office came out and rushed out the front office door. Jacob stopped long enough to tell Jody to get her pen, paper, and recorder and follow them. As they rushed down the hall, Jacob called the guard on his cell phone and asked him to have the media meet them in Statuary

Hall. On the way to the Capitol Building by way of the underground subway, he called the Intelligence people for an update. Finally at the door of Statuary Hall, he stopped to take several deep breaths.

The reporters covering Capitol Hill were assembled and had quickly put up their lights and microphones. A stream of senators and congresspeople were standing in the Hall as well as in the Rotunda waiting to see what was going to be said. Jacob stepped up to the podium and gazed around at the group before looking into the camera.

"Good morning, everyone. By now you have all heard that our country has been attacked by terrorists. Radioactive bombs have been detonated across our nation. I've been in contact with our Intelligence people, and the President and Vice President have been taken to a safe place. We will give updates to their location and wellbeing as more news comes in. Senator Lucy Katrin, Senator Justin Pebbles, Congressman Jack Shiver, and I will be working with other members of Congress on the way forward. Our first concern is, of course, to get citizens out of the affected areas and then blockade those regions off. We must ensure people stay in areas that are not radioactive at this time. Our military will be inspecting each affected place to ensure no more bombs were hidden to be detonated. Please stay where you are until it is determined what areas may still be unsafe. Although we know the places that have been attacked, we don't know if any others are going to be targeted.

The radioactive material dispersed by the bombs is being carried by the wind to other cities and towns as well. This will increase the areas of evacuation, so if you are in or near an affected region at this time, please stay inside until you are told where to go.

We are searching for the culprits and will report to you as soon as they are caught. Please stay tuned to your news station to keep informed. Thank you!"

The media began to fire questions at the House Speaker as soon as he finished his speech. Jacob just waved, and he and those around him left the Hall. As they distanced themselves from the others, Jacob turned to his group, "It's done. We'll wait a few hours and then go back to update the public again. In the meantime, we'll get ahold of our contacts at the CIA and FBI for updates." The four went back to their own offices to calm down and get prepared for the next step.

Everyone in the Capitol came out in the hallways talking to those around them in astonishment. How could any of this happen without the FBI or CIA knowing about it? Multiple bombs in multiple areas deployed and no warning. Something seemed awfully strange to those who listened to Jacob's speech.

A few of the senators and congresspeople went to Jacob's office to see what else he knew. Jody was already back at her desk staring at her computer in disbelief when a mob from Congress entered the office and just bypassed her going straight in to see Jacob. Senator Stu Seagly was among them, and they all started speaking at once.

"Calm down everyone," Jacob held up his hand. The President and Vice President have been moved to a safe location for now. They were visiting a site in Baltimore when the bombs went off. Unfortunately, they were together, and we haven't been in contact with them yet."

Stu spoke up, "How could this have happened? How bad were the radiation blasts? Where were our intelligence reports? Why didn't we know this was going to happen?"

Jacob scanned the people demanding answers, "I don't know all of the answers yet. I'll let you all know when I find out." He finally got everyone to go back to their offices to wait for further information.

After collecting himself and getting focused, he called Jody in. "Jody, I'll need you to stay in the office until we have more information. Go down and get something to eat and make yourself comfortable." She smiled and left his office wondering if Jamie was with the President somewhere.

Heading down to the cafeteria, she pulled her phone out of her pocket and called Jamie. Her sister's phone rang, and finally the voicemail kicked in. "Where is she!"

Jody answered calls continuously, and about one-thirty Jacob called her into his office and said he would again address the public from Statuary Hall at two o'clock. He wanted her to be completely ready to ensure every word everyone said was recorded, and any actions not recordable should be a written record.

The media again waited for an update, and Jacob's group was there to stand behind him for support. He was getting tired and annoyed, but he smiled and stepped to the podium professionally like politicians train themselves to do.

"Good afternoon, everyone. We have received updated information concerning the attacks on our country today. Ten terrorists from Asia have been caught. The FBI is still searching for more perpetrators who participated in the bombings.

We still do not have the exact level of radiation that was dispersed, but it is believed to be one of the deadliest radiation types. So in order to keep our citizens safe, we are putting these directives into place.

The country is now under martial law. All private businesses, state and local agencies, social and volunteer services, religious worship and activities, and some federal government offices will be closed. Every person in an affected area must travel to a safe area. The National Guard and military will assist.

Because of the radiation, all schools will be closed. We must keep educating our children through this time of tragedy, so children age five to eighteen will enter government camps where they will be educated and live in dormitories without fear of harm. The government will take existing buildings to create these camps, so they should be set up quickly. The children will continue to learn and will stay at these camps until such time as regular school can resume. The military will pick up the children and take them to their designated camp once the sites are established.

Our food supply will dwindle quickly as thousands of acres of farmland were in the targeted areas and food cannot be grown in radiation-soaked soil. To this end, your Administration will ensure food is shipped from other countries to make up for all that will be lost here. With the need of assuring all food obtained by our citizens is radiation-free, we are setting up temporary distribution centers in safe areas so food and other essentials can be obtained immediately. The Federal Emergency Management Agency or FEMA will manage these sites with the assistance of the National Guard and military.

We have not determined yet how many terrorists are still at large. In an effort to secure our nation and keep our citizens safe, part of the Pentagon's mission will change to monitoring the people in the interior of the United States to assist the FBI. This will continue as long as necessary to ensure we capture all of the culprits who participated in the bombings and help to safeguard against more catastrophes of this type in the future.

These requirements will stay in effect until such time as they are no longer necessary. We appreciate your adherence to these directives. Thank you."

The media then went crazy asking questions. "Why are you setting the rules?" "Where's the President?" "Who are the terrorists?" "When will you know martial law is no longer needed?" Jacob and his group walked away without answering any questions.

Lucy followed Jacob back to his office. "We have to get Congress together and tell them what we know and why we are doing what we're doing. Everyone up here is in the dark, and it's starting to cause lots of problems."

"Alright," Jacob agreed. "Have them announce that Congress will meet in the House Chamber at four o'clock this afternoon. I'll do the talking."

After Lucy left, Jody went into the Speaker's office. "Congressman Peterson, I need to make sure my sister is alright. I think you remember she works for the President's Chief of Staff."

"Yes Jody, if I hear anything I'll let you know. We'll be addressing Congress at four, so please be ready."

Jody nodded and walked out of his office frustrated. She tried Jamie's number again, but there was no answer. She decided to call Gregg. "Gregg, it's Jody. I can only talk for a few minutes. Have you heard from Jamie?"

"Nope," Gregg told her. "Do you know where she is? I was playing ball with the guys this morning, and I just now got home from a meeting."

Jody sighed, "You better turn the TV on. Lots of bombs went off across the country, and the President, VP, and their staff are somewhere. We haven't been told where they are, and we haven't gotten a list yet of who was on that tour. Watch the TV and see what orders Peterson just gave out. I'm sure they'll be repeated multiple times. I have to go. I'll call back as soon as I can."

All of the senators and congresspeople who were in the building congregated in the House Chamber. They were talking among themselves about all that had happened so far. Jacob got to the Chamber and went to the podium. Quickly, many of the members started asking questions. Jacob held up his hand for silence.

"Please be seated, everyone. I know you have all heard about the attacks on our country this morning. I'm sure you also heard that ten terrorists have been caught by the FBI."

Senator Steven Blackbone spoke loudly from the back of the room. "Who decided to make all of the demands that you announced at two o'clock? Where is the FBI on locating the rest of the terrorists? With all of the bombs that went off, there has to be a lot more terrorists out there."

Jacob nodded. "I know you all have many questions, and I am here to answer anything that I can at this point. As House Speaker, I decided to take these actions from the information I was given. Senator Lucy Katrin, Congressman Jack Shiver, and Senator Justin Pebbles have been working closely with me. We have not been able to reach the President yet, so as soon as we do, we will let you know. It is known that there are more terrorists out there, and the FBI is still looking for them."

Constant conversation was coming from all parts of the room. Senator Alice Schmidt spoke up next. "I think we should spread the responsibilities out among many of us. We should get into committees and make decisions on the area we are to watch over."

"I understand how everyone feels," Jacob responded. "Once we have more information and understand the situation fully, we will all get together and make decisions jointly. Until then, we must act quickly when new information comes in. But during this period, please consider new actions that can be taken to protect our citizens. That is all I have to share at this time. If you have any more questions, please contact one of my staffers or one of the others I told you I have been working closely with. Thank you."

Jacob stepped down from the podium, and several senators approached him with more questions. He stood there and answered what he could. The others were in groups discussing what was said and what was being done. Most of the people in the room were not happy.

Finally, the Speaker got back to his office with his three comrades. Jody followed and stopped at her desk watching them fade into the next room. Jacob stuck his head out the door and told Jody she could leave for the night. As he went back into his office, his cell phone rang. "Peterson here."

"It's Randy. What do you want me to do with the President and his staff?"

"Nothing," Jacob said emphatically. "He has to stay unavailable until we get everything set up."

Randy sarcastically told him a bit of new information, "By the way, did you hear Congressman Handler died? I was talking to his assistant, and it seems Handler told a reporter most every dirty deed he and other politicians did throughout the years. Could make a big mess for you."

"Who was the reporter?" Peterson asked.

"Phil Bender was the one who recorded the old man I was told." Randy almost laughed out loud.

"I'll take care of that. Don't call me again; I'll contact you," Jacob ended the call. "You guys better get home and get some sleep," he told his conspirators. Everyone left his office except for Lucy.

"What was the reporter business about?"

"Seems old man Handler invited a reporter over to record his sins before he died. Told this guy a lot of the dirty and illegal actions he took while in office as well as some things he did working with other politicians," Peterson was furious.

"What are you going to do?" Lucy asked concerned.

"I'll take care of it, don't worry," he said smiling at her. She left and Jacob started thinking while he stared at the pencil he kept tapping on the desk. A little while later, he picked up his phone and called an old friend. "Hi Rick, this is Jacob. Got a job for you to do."

Lucy got home and turned on the TV to see what was being said about the activities at the Capitol. She smiled as she headed for the shower, because most news stations assured the people that the Speaker of the House was doing exactly what needed to be done to keep everyone safe. The reporters told the public not to ask questions but follow the decisions that government had made. "Perfect," she thought. "Keep following the decisions the government makes

49

without asking any questions." She laughed as she began to take her clothes off.

The next morning, Phil's boss got out of bed and stretched as he noticed how beautifully the sun was shining. It looked like a lovely day outside. He went to the kitchen to make coffee and then stuck his head out the front door to retrieve the paper while waving good morning to his neighbor. Sitting at his kitchen table, he started to enjoy the news of the day. As he turned to page seven, he saw an article about a man who was shot trying to escape the police. The article said Philip Bender was wanted on charges of espionage and had fired a gun at the police causing them to shoot him. He died instantly. Bob got tears in his eyes for the friend he had known for so long. "Oh dear God, they found out about Handler and killed him."

Bob called Gregg and told him what had happened. "Do you still have the recorder he gave you?" Bob asked. "I've got the one from the night Handler died."

Gregg was shaken, "Yeah, I have the recorder. Listen Bob, they will be looking for these recorders, so I'll come and get the one you have. Either Handler's assistant or that doctor made sure someone knew about this. After I leave your place, you better get out of there buddy. Hop a plane or train and go stay at a hotel somewhere under a different name for a while."

"Okay," Bob said in disbelief. "Wow, I didn't see this coming."

CHAPTER FIVE

After Gregg hung up from talking to Bob, he called Jody. "Hey Jody, have they gotten the list of people who were with the President? Jamie hasn't called and hasn't been home, so she must have been with them. I've called her a dozen times, and she never answers her phone. I talked to a lady at the White House and she wouldn't tell me anything."

"I can't get her either," Jody said disheartened. "She must have been with them, and no, we haven't gotten that list or been told where they are. Peterson said they were in a safe place, but I don't know how he knows that and I don't trust him."

Gregg didn't say anything for a minute, then he replied, "I've got some buddies on the inside, and I gave them a call to see if they know anything. Still waiting for them to get back with me. Shit this is getting way out of hand, and whoever is behind this is going to work fast to get what they want. Hey what's Peterson doing announcing all of the new rules? Who gave him the power to do that?"

"I know," she sounded like she was going to cry. "I'm watching my computer for new emails. I don't know what anybody is doing, but I think Peterson has a plan. I'm taking my computer home with me to watch the correspondence trail and see if anything comes across. Right now, people are so afraid they'll do anything. Just a minute, an email from Peterson just went out to everyone on the Hill. It says they believe the President and his group have been taken hostage. Oh no!!!"

"Yeah, something's terribly wrong. Our FBI should have seen this coming. I'll call you as soon as I know anything." Just as Gregg hung up, he got another call.

"Hi Gregg, it's Chuck."

"Hi Chuck! What in the hell is going on? I can't find my wife, and she works under the Chief of Staff at the White House!" Gregg got angrier as he talked.

"Lots of troubles, buddy," Chuck sympathized. "We found the President, but we don't know who is with him. The longer this goes on the scarier it gets."

Gregg paused, "Have they caught any more terrorists yet?"

"Yeah," his friend answered, "they got a dozen more. But there are still more out there."

"Is this an inside job, Chuck?"

Chuck stalled for a minute but couldn't lie to his Service brother, "Looks like it. I've got to go, buddy. I'll call you back if any new information comes in."

Gregg hung up and clicked the TV on. The media was in multiple cities showing the impact of the bombs that were released. Anita, one of the newscasters, spoke to the public.

"We are on the outskirts of Philadelphia, and this part is a high population region that had multiple detonations. We've been told sixty-eight people were killed in this section alone and there may be more. The first responders have no idea how many have been injured, but we are all lucky that our government is on top of things and taking care of those targeted. Here comes a local person who experienced a blast. Sir, can you tell me what you saw when the explosion went off?"

The man looked completely stunned but stopped to answer the lady, "It was like the fury of hell. Explosions going off all over." He suddenly got tears in his eyes as he started to move on.

"Did you hear that the public is supposed to go to safe areas?" the newscaster asked gently.

"Yes," the man stopped and turned back to her. "I intend to do that as soon as I get my whole family together and get some food to take."

"Go to a safe place, sir. The Federal Emergency Management Agency will bring you what you need. Be patient and let them do their job." The newscaster turned back to the camera, "And to the rest of you out there, go to a safe place. Don't go into the radioactive areas for any reason. FEMA will bring you what you need and keep you informed."

Gregg remembered Bob and got up quickly. He shut off the TV and grabbed his keys before heading out the door.

At the Capitol, Jacob was again in Statuary Hall preparing to address the nation. People in the Capitol crowded around behind him so the public could see how concerned they were. Jacob began his speech.

"Dear Americans, I am here to report to you that more terrorists have been caught and are being interrogated. We now know that the President, Vice President, and their staff have been taken hostage. The FBI knows their location, and negotiations are being held. We will keep you updated on this situation through the news media or through Capitol Hill briefings.

To update you on our progress in affected towns, we are continuing to move all citizens in the radioactive areas to shelters in safe places. Food and water distribution are our first concerns after any needed medical care has been given. The National Guard and Army are assisting FEMA in ensuring these items are available.

Please be patient and do as you are asked from those there to assist. We all must work together to make this a success. Thank you for your support."

Most people were glued to their TVs. After Jacob's speech, responders were shown on screens helping the injured, and search teams were carrying the deceased in body bags. Homes and businesses appeared that had been destroyed, and gas lines were shown on fire as multiple gas explosions had occurred in different areas. People moving out of the radiation areas were cautioned to avoid the streets where gas lines had been on fire since the bombings took place.

A newsman updates the people. "Fires are still raging, and the military is going from house to house moving people to shelters. Even those who refuse to leave are being forced to go to relocation spots. As people are moved out, radioactive areas are being shut off, and military personnel are guarding the regions to keep people away. It has been reported that many more towns are receiving radioactive fallout with the wind. These areas will have to be evacuated as well. We can see FEMA and the military bringing in food and water to ration to the public. Lines are forming so people can at least have one meal before they are shipped off to another place. There is a great deal of chaos out here, so please stay safe everyone and do what you are asked to do to make things go smoothly. We'll continue to keep you updated as new information comes in."

That night, Jody was at home listening to the news. She didn't believe anything her boss said, and she started scanning his correspondence on the computer she brought home. "Peterson forgot I have access to his text messages. If I look through those, I could lose my job, but Jamie is more important."

She began to read his texts out loud, "Jacob, I can't believe how smoothly things are going so far. Citizens are letting us do what we want, we are backed by the military, and the President is gone. Good work!!!" Jody was disgusted, "Nice email, Lucy. Here's one from Jack Shiver saying things are going good!!! Within a few weeks, we'll be running everything!" Jody shut her computer off. She started to cry and decided to call Gregg.

"Hi Gregg, it's Jody. Wanted to tell you what I found out. Not good."

"What is it Jody? Is it about Jamie?" Gregg was anxious.

"I think so," Jody said half-heartedly. "One senator is glad citizens are letting them do what they want. They have the military backing them, and it said the President is gone! Another text said they'll be running everything in a couple of weeks!!! I can't believe he left those two messages and didn't get rid of them. All the rest for the last week he deleted."

Gregg didn't want to upset Jody anymore, but he felt like he had to be honest with her. "I talked to a couple of buddies on the inside and found out some things too, Jody. I don't think they've harmed anyone in the President's group. They will but haven't yet. Once Peterson has full power, I'm afraid all of those involved with the top-down takeover we are watching will get rid of everyone who is with the President."

"What can I do?" Jody was almost hysterical. "I have to do something!"

"I don't know yet," he felt helpless. "Keep an eye on what Peterson does, and we'll figure this out. Jamie will be alright. Watch and stay focused!"

As Jody hung up, she began to feel better knowing Gregg was going to keep looking for Jamie. She knew everything would be okay somehow, so she decided to pull herself together and keep her eyes open. Working together they could do anything.

Confusion and chaos ruled throughout the country. Everyday those in Congress were trying to get a sense of what was going on. A few had already figured out where this was headed, and they weren't happy with it.

Senator Steven Blackbone caught Peterson in a hallway of the Capitol one day and started to position himself in the hierarchy he knew was coming. "Hey Jacob, I think I would be a good candidate for the head person over all contracts for any type of construction you think we might need. I have experience in that, and I know many good contractors for many different types of building projects."

Peterson was not in the mood, "I haven't started on that yet, Steve. I'll keep you in mind." Peterson walked away tired of all the endless tasks they had to attend to so they could get where they wanted to be.

Leaving the Capitol, he headed for Lucy's office. Once there, he bypassed her assistant and walked right in to see her. He shook his head, "How are we going to get rid of all the wannabes out there? We're going to have to slowly get rid of more than three quarters of them."

Lucy smiled trying to lighten up the conversation, "Just take your time. You are the boss now, so take it a step at a time so there is no revolt. As soon as we get all of those who refused to do things our way settled into the new world we're making, the hard part will be over. Think things through carefully."

Jacob nodded, "I'll see you tonight at our place. You can work the tension out of my body." He smiled and left.

Gregg was glad Bob had packed and was on his way to a city that hadn't been affected by the blasts. He would keep in contact with him in case he heard something. Gregg continued to call his buddies who were still in the Service, but only a couple could tell him anything. He decided to call Mark.

"Hi Mark, it's Gregg. Do you remember Bob and Phil who had the recordings of Handler?"

"Yeah, did they get some more information?" Mark wondered.

"Yes, but the regime had Phil killed. Shot in the head. I went over to Bob's to get that last recorder, and then he left D.C. to hide out under a different name. Peterson's henchmen will be looking for those recordings, because someone told them Phil had those discussions with Handler. Have you been listening to the news?"

"Yeah," Mark answered, "the Marines are really messing this thing up. If we were still in special ops, the President and his group would be sitting in the White House right now."

"No, the Marines aren't screwing up. They are being told to stand down." Gregg spoke very quietly. "My wife is in that group, Mark. We know Peterson and his cohorts are filthy, and they aren't going to do anything good with the President or the people with him."

"We can get her out, Gregg," Mark assured his buddy. "We just have to find out where they are. Look, I'll call the guys and we'll meet at Trooper's Bar in a couple of hours."

Gregg walked into Trooper's and didn't see anyone, so he sat at the bar and ordered a drink. A few minutes later Mark, Leo, Max, and Gunman walked in. They each gave Gregg a bear hug, and the group walked over to a table.

"Okay guys," Mark was deadly serious, "it's time to get down to business. We all heard the news, and the special op Marines have been told to stand down for the hostage situation. That means the government is behind this, and Gregg's wife is one of the hostages."

"How the hell did that happen?" Leo looked at Gregg.

Gregg shook his head, "She works for the White House Chief of Staff. She must have been with them on their tour in Baltimore. None of that group knew bombings were planned which is something the FBI should have known and reported to the White House.

Anna

"That's right," Leo agreed. "It isn't possible for the bad guys to have walked into the Baltimore tour with all the secret service around. They had to be escorted in."

"What's the FBI doing in Baltimore?" Max asked.

Gregg shrugged.

"Okay," Mark began, "this is what we're going to do. Max, you have contacts with the FBI and Pentagon. Find out where they are. Leo, you have contacts in the FBI and CIA, so find out who has them. See if they're our folks or foreign terrorists. Gunman, you need to work with Max, and when you find out where they are, you need to make a route in. Gregg, you need to stay calm and let us work this out. You're too close to the subject, and you know how that can affect an operation."

Everyone agreed to the plan and that they would meet back at Trooper's the next day at the same time.

Gregg went home and said a small prayer that Jamie and the others would be alright and everything would work out for the country. He paced around the house having a hard time waiting. Waiting to see what plan he and his buddies could come up with, waiting for Jamie to come home, waiting for the chaos across the country to come to an end. He finally decided to call Jody and see what she was doing.

"Hi Jody."

"Oh Gregg, I'm so glad you called. They still haven't given any information on where Jamie is or who has her."

"I know," Gregg was sympathetic. He loved Jamie, but he also realized that Jody was her twin sister. The bond they shared would be very hard to lose if something happened to his wife. "I met with some of my buddies today, and they're sure we can get her out as soon as we find out where they are."

"How do we do that?" Jody was getting more upset.

"My friends have contacts on the inside and are going to find out where they are and who has them. Don't worry, Jody, we'll find her and get her back. I'm working with the best of the best on this, and if there is any way to get Jamie back, we'll do it."

Jody calmed down a little. "I know you will, Gregg. I know you love Jamie and you'll do anything to get her back. If you need help from me, please let me know. Thanks." She hung up believing there was still hope she would see her sister again.

56

The next day, all of the guys met back at Trooper's. Gregg was on edge, and Mark noticed that right away. "Gregg, you have to trust us. I know you're upset, but we'll do our best to get her back."

"I know you will," Gregg smiled at his buddies. "I'm lucky to have friends like you who are the top layer of any special operation."

Mark smiled back and turned to Max, "What did you find out, Max?"

"They've got them in an apartment building by the Baltimore docks. There are lots of bars and apartment buildings around, so that means there will be a lot of civilians walking around and in the complexes. There's no FBI to be seen in the area, and that is very weird. I would have thought they would have agents surrounding the place, but they were ordered to stay away. Negotiations are going on, but I don't know who is doing the talking. Not even sure what kind of discussions they are."

Leo smirked, "Yeah, and the people holding the hostages are our people not terrorists. Not sure if they're experts or thugs, but they aren't foreign people. Those around the country who detonated the bombs might have come from other places, but the people directing this plan and holding the captives are ours. Whoever hired these guys told them nothing bad would happen to them. Yeah, right. As soon as the officials know their plan has worked and those they hired are no longer needed, they will be taken care of along with the hostages."

Mark changed the subject quickly and asked Gunman what he planned out. Gunman laid a map on the table and unrolled it. "There are a couple of ways in. If they're really experts and not punks off the street, we're going to have a hard time getting in without being seen."

Gregg put his hand on Gunman's, "But it's possible?"

All of the men looked at Gregg, and they knew he wasn't thinking straight. They looked at each other and understood they had to keep Gregg away from any plan they came up with because he wasn't able to focus. Any raid they went on to get the people back would be in danger because he was not looking at the details. They smiled at him and went back to their discussion.

"Did you get a route marked out for us?" Mark asked Gunman.

"We've got two ways in. One way is to come down from the roof into a room above them and then go down and storm in. The building is old and has stairways that will be dark, squeaky, and unused for the most part. The other way is to wait for the change of guard and grab the new guys coming in. I think that is probably the best option. They won't know why or care if personnel has changed for some reason. If we can disarm and make the new shift powerless, there will be less gun activity and less chance of hurting innocent people or those being held hostage."

Gregg tapped his fingers on the table, "If they're in that type of nasty hole in the wall, they aren't planning on letting them talk about it. We don't know the timeline of the masterminds, so the sooner we get up there and get this done the better."

They all agreed. Mark set up the next meeting, "Okay, we'll meet at Gregg's house tomorrow at two to finish up the plans. Think these things over good tonight so we don't miss anything. We'll get up there day after tomorrow.

The next morning, Jody walked into her office and heard yelling coming from Peterson's office. She heard a man telling Peterson that he was tired of babysitting the idiots from the White House. She could hear Peterson talking but couldn't hear what he said. The man started talking at a lower volume, so she only heard mumbling from that point and couldn't make words out of any of the sounds.

After a few minutes of listening to indistinguishable words, the man she saw before walked angrily out of his office slamming the door and gave her a dirty look. He threw a gum wrapper in her wastebasket and stormed out the front office door. Jody waited for Peterson to come out or to call her in, but he didn't do either. Her phone rang, "Congressman Peterson's office."

Gregg was on the line, "It's me. Call me from your cell phone."

Jody said okay and hung up. She glanced back at Peterson's office door, and it was still shut tight. She pressed Gregg's name and her phone dialed the number.

"Listen," he told her, "my friends found out where Jamie and the others are and who has them. We're going to have to go in after them; it's the only way. We're meeting at two today to finish up the plans, and then we're going in to get her."

"Gregg, when I came in this morning there was a man in Peterson's office yelling about being tired of babysitting the idiots from the White House. He was so angry when he left all he did was give me a dirty look. I'm really afraid for them!"

"Calm down," he told her. "Do you know who he was?"

"I took a picture of him the other day when he left Peterson's office. He looked mean or just not right, so I followed him out of the building and snapped a picture. I hope he's nowhere near Jamie!" she exclaimed. "I can send the picture to you if that will help."

"Send the picture, Jody. Maybe one of us will know who he is. I'll talk to you later and let you know what's going on." Gregg hung up and waited for the picture to come through. Once he got it, he kept staring at it because he knew he had seen this man before.

At two o'clock Max knocked on the door and the four of them walked into Gregg's house. They went into the kitchen and sat at the table. Gregg got the picture up on his phone and passed it around, "Do any of you know this guy?"

Leo nodded the second he saw the picture. "That's a guy from the FBI."

Gunman took the phone back and looked at the picture again, "So he quit the FBI and is making money taking hostages. Great government people we have."

Gregg looked at him, "Are you sure?"

Leo looked at the picture again, "Oh, that is a guy from the FBI. I remember working with him when we were still inside. He helped the special op teams with information that was needed to plan out operations. Always seemed unfriendly and acted like he was smarter than everyone else. Didn't care for him."

"Well he was in Peterson's office today yelling about babysitting the people from the White House," Gregg told them. "He has to be the one overseeing the hostages. Have you got the plan all laid out and the timeframe?"

Mark answered, "If we can, we're going to get the relief guys as they go in. We've got all the gear that we'll need, so tomorrow morning we're going up and checking out the building and watch the change of guard. That way we'll know exactly how they do it. One of us will dress up as a vagrant and walk in behind them so we know exactly what floor and room they're in. We'll also have the times of the changes and be able to set up and be ready just before they get there."

"Where are we meeting tomorrow?" Gregg asked nonchalantly.

"Sorry buddy," Max gave him a half smile. "You're not going."

"Bullshit, she's my wife," Gregg slammed his fist on the table.

"Look it," Leo said nicely, "we'll take care of her. You'll make too many mistakes just for that reason."

"Well make damn sure nothing happens to her," Gregg looked around the table very seriously.

The guys looked at each other knowing their strategy would save or sacrifice every hostage being held in the building.

Anna

The next morning Max, Mark, Leo, and Gunman pulled up by the place holding the hostages. They parked in-between a moving truck and a large car so they were partially hidden from view and began to watch the building. People dressed very shabbily sat outside many of the structures up and down the street. A few couples came out, and a few of those had babies or little kids with them. There were older kids playing ball on one of the side streets, and some little girls were playing jump rope. Quite a bit of drinking was going on, and they saw people taking drugs right out in the open. No FBI or police were seen anywhere.

They saw four men dressed in suits go up the building steps and disappear into the entranceway about three forty-five. Suddenly they saw a man dressed in new clothes walk out of the building, and he started to look around.

Max lifted his small binoculars, "That's got to be one of the guys who is being replaced. It's three-fifty, so the change must come at four." In the next ten minutes they saw three more guys like the first stroll down the steps. They all got into the same car and left.

"The relief guys got here about fifteen minutes before the change so the previous shift could update them." Gunman said. "The next shift will be at midnight then, so Leo you'll be ready to follow them in to see where they go."

Leo nodded, "So once I know where they are, we'll go in and get them?"

"No," Mark said. "That's too quick. I want to know for sure that the guards all change shifts that way. We'll watch them tonight and tomorrow, and then we'll know how they do it each time for sure. Tomorrow night we go in and get them."

Gunman agreed, "We're going to have to split up. Two of us can get something to eat and get some sleep, and the other two can watch the building. We'll change about three in the morning. That way everybody will get some kind of sleep."

"I'll take the first shift with Gunman," Leo smiled. "You two go get some grub and sleep and we'll see you later.

Leo was dressed and ready for the midnight shift. He had already gotten out of the car and was standing by the building with a bottle of liquor in his hand. As the new guards went into the building, Leo followed them acting as if he was drunk. He stayed a little behind and went slowly so he wouldn't attract any attention. The men went to the fifth floor, and then Leo saw each of them go to a different room. He went down a couple of flights of

60

stairs and sat on a step pretending to drink waiting for the guards that were being replaced to leave. They passed him on their way down and didn't give Leo a second look. He waited about ten minutes then weaved his way out of the building. Standing against the structure, he looked around to make certain they were gone.

"I was afraid they were standing out here talking," Leo told Gunman as he slid back into the car. "They're on the fifth floor, but each one of them went to a different room. So how are we going to handle that?" Leo looked at Gunman and knew the ex-Marine would have a plan.

Mark and Max got to the apartment building just before three in the morning. Gunman told them the problem they had, "Looks like we're each going to have to take a room, boys. Leo followed them to the fifth floor, but they all went to different rooms on the right side of the hall, and we have no idea who is in each of the rooms. It'll be better if we go up after the midnight shift leaves. The guards will be more relaxed at that late hour."

"Do we have enough gear for four rooms?" Max asked.

Gunman smiled, "Yeah, I brought extra. We'll each be armed and have a smoke bomb. We each take a door and at the same time break it in and throw the smoke bomb in. We'll have masks which they won't have, and that will give us time to take the guys down or shoot them. One way or the other we all know how this plays out, so we should be fine."

They all agreed to the plan and were certain it would work. Being in special ops gave them nerves of steel, and they were ready.

"Gunman, Leo, go get some rest. We'll meet you at our room around noon and get some sleep, and then we'll get prepared," Mark smiled at his buddies.

That night at eleven thirty the Marines were dressed in dark clothes and had their weapons on their hips. Mark looked at each of them, "Ready?" They nodded. "Good, we'll wait in the car until the relief shift has gone in and we see the other guys leave. About ten minutes after that we go in so we get them before they finish checking the hostages and the room situation. That should give us the edge of surprise. Have your smoke bombs ready."

The group watched from the car and saw the new shift go in. A few minutes later, the other shift had all come out and had gotten in a car and left. As the four looked around, they didn't see any tenants sitting on any building steps or walking down the street. The lights were on in different apartments, and they could see a shadow by the window of one of the target rooms. Ten minutes later the four quietly left the car and started walking towards the target building.

As they walked across the street, they saw a bright flash and were blown back against the vehicle. Mark and Gunman were knocked out, and Leo and Max pulled them away from the raging fire that had erupted in the building.

"Dear God Almighty! They're gone; they killed them!" Leo cried out.

CHAPTER SIX

At two in the morning in Peterson's office, Lucy and Jacob sat watching TV. They were waiting for the news that the ones they wanted out of the way were gone.

Lucy smiled at Jacob, "What will we tell the media about the President and Vice President?"

"I'll tell them what we're told by our Intelligence," Jacob smiled back. "But first, we have to hear the news then make certain the experts verify. After that, we get rid of the people in Baltimore. I expect it may take a week or so to get back confirmed results of who was in that building, so we're just going to have to play along until we have the report in our hands."

"I hope to hell no one in Baltimore told anyone else what they're doing," Lucy looked concerned. She had worked in D.C. long enough to know people liked to take politicians down. Getting dirt on someone who worked on Capitol Hill was something they all tried to do, and this type of information would ruin their careers for good. Lucy was afraid that someone else on the Hill had news of what was going on and was tracking down proof.

Jacob patted her hand, "Don't worry. Even if they did talk to someone else, they can't connect it to us. We have the FBI and all of the military behind us to take care of anyone who dares accuse us of anything."

Just then, a news anchor appeared on TV with a news update. Jacob and Lucy stopped talking and listened to what the man on the screen had to say.

"These are the latest headlines. D.C. saw multiple protests from people who had come from all parts of the country. The protesters continued to voice objections to the directives Congress made since the bombs detonated spewing radiation in large areas. Many are worried that government is overstepping its role, and most of those we spoke to were demanding that they be able to return to their normal life. Others were adamant that the military will never take their children. The protesters were disbanded by military police bringing our nation's Capital back into order.

Following the direction from our government, businesses have closed down, but very few centers are set up yet to distribute food, water, and other necessities. National Guard members have been riding around in trucks to distribute what they have hoping they can reach all who are without.

In New York, a fire is currently destroying an apartment building. No reports of casualties have been received yet, but there is a great deal of fear that the fire will spread to adjacent buildings.

In Baltimore, a building was destroyed by some type of explosion. It is not clear yet if this was another terrorist bomb or there was some other cause. There is also no report concerning deaths or injuries."

Jacob stood up, "There it is, so now we wait to see who they find in there. I hope it doesn't take them too long. There are lots of laws I am ready to sign."

The phone started ringing, and Jacob answered. "Hello."

An FBI agent was on the other end of the line, "Sir, the explosion in Baltimore was where the President and his group were being held. The fire department is extinguishing the flames, but it could be a couple of days before they can get in there to see how many people were involved. It might possibly be a week before they know who was in the building for sure."

"Alright, thank you. Please keep me updated." Jacob hung up and smiled at Lucy. "Okay, we'll update the public later this morning. We can't touch those guys until we make certain it's done. Hopefully it won't take them too long."

Lucy got behind Jacob and began to rub his neck. He sat in his chair relaxed as she continued to go down to his shoulders and down his chest.

"That feels good," Jacob took her hand and brought her around the chair.

Lucy kissed him gently, "Shouldn't we go to our favorite hotel and celebrate?"

Across town, Gregg was at his house pacing back and forth. He knew his buddies were going to go in for the hostages that night and was afraid something would go wrong. "Jamie needs to be home, God. I love her and need her, and I don't want her to be afraid or harmed by the thugs who have them. Please help my buddies get her out safely!" He continued walking back and forth not knowing what else to do until he got the call that his wife was with his friends and heading home. "I should be there. I should be helping them, and what if Jamie gets hurt when they go in to get them? I won't be there! What if something happens to her and I never see her again?"

The phone rang, and Gregg jumped and then picked it up. "Mark! What's going on? You guys getting ready to go into the building soon?"

Mark waited a few seconds, "Gregg." His friend broke down and Gregg could hear him struggle to talk.

"What happened, Mark?" Gregg almost shouted into the phone.

He cleared his throat and answered his friend, "We were getting ready to go in. Had everything we needed and had watched the place so we knew the routine. Just as we got out of the car and started walking across the street to the building, a bomb went off."

Gregg gasped, "Did you get inside? Did you get Jamie?"

"No," Mark answered, "there wasn't a chance. It was as if the whole building ignited instantaneously, and every door and lower window was too hot to try to enter."

"Dear God, she's still in there!" Gregg shouted. "I'm on my way up!"

"Gregg, stay where you are," Mark tried to talk calmly. "One of us will be watching every minute. You can't do anything here. Please!"

"Alright," he agreed, "but you have to call me every hour and let me know what's going on. I have to get her back Mark!"

"I know buddy," Mark almost started crying. "Look, this isn't over. We'll find her, and we'll make sure those who took her are put away for life. They won't be able to hide."

At that moment, Jody was just getting up from trying to sleep. She picked up a book but couldn't concentrate, so she laid it down. TV didn't interest her, so she looked at her phone and once again pressed Jamie's number. Nothing! Laying the phone on the couch, Jody headed to the kitchen to get something to eat. Then, she heard the phone ringing. Certain they had found her sister, she ran back to the couch and answered. It was a wrong number, so patiently Jody told the caller they had reached the wrong person. She was so disappointed she dropped her phone back on the couch and went to the kitchen.

The phone rang again, and somehow she knew the call was from her brother-in-law, "What's wrong, Gregg?"

He didn't know what to say because he was still in shock himself. When he didn't respond, Jody asked again.

"The building we think Jamie was in blew up. The firefighters are working to put out the fire, and then they'll be able to tell who was inside." He started to break down.

Jody became hysterical, so Gregg shook off his fears and tried to get her to focus, "Jody, calm down. We really don't know anything yet. Let's just wait and see what happens. As soon as I find anything out, I'll let you know." After a minute he said, "Okay?"

She started talking with quiet anger, "I want to know now! I just don't feel like she's dead, but if she is those bastards on the Hill killed her. They'll get away with it too just like they always get away with breaking the law and making special rules for themselves. Oh, they'll have lots of special committees looking into it and calling witnesses and making a big production of how tuned in they are to the people. They'll accomplish nothing as usual, and the episode will be forgotten while they move on to kill our country. I'll talk to you later Gregg."

Jody hung up and Gregg stared at his phone wanting to believe that Jamie wasn't dead, but he was pretty sure Jody was wrong. How could this happen in America? Then Gregg started getting mad too as he thought about everything Jody had said. "We'll just see about that."

Later that morning, Jacob got ready to address the nation. Only he and Lucy knew what the FBI found out the night before, so he understood that there would be great distress throughout the country as well as with the media and the other people in Congress.

The different media stations were all set up waiting for the update to the nation. They expected to hear that the FBI had found out some new information and had apprehended the kidnappers finding the President and his group alive and well. An update on the attacks on the country was also expected.

Jacob stood at the podium in Statuary Hall surrounded by his group and others from Congress. The House Speaker began to address the public.

"Good morning, everyone. We were told early this morning that the building where the President and his group were being held was the building in Baltimore that exploded. We do not have verification of who was in that building yet, and we will update everyone as soon as we have more information. Right now, we ask that you all pray for the President, Vice President, and all of the staff who were taken hostage. Thank you."

The Congressional members on the podium turned to leave, and the reporters started to yell out questions they knew everyone wanted answers to. Jacob decided to answer a few of them, so he turned back to those with the microphones.

"When will they know who was in the building?"

Jacob answered, "We are hoping in a few days. The firefighters have to ensure the remains of the building are safe to enter so victims inside can be found and identified. It was quite a large apartment building, but we are hoping the structure has cooled down enough and the experts are able to enter very soon.

The next reporter shouted out a question, "Doesn't the White House have a list of people who were with the President?"

"We haven't been given that list yet," Jacob looked regretful. "I will ask again, and hopefully we will get a list of everyone."

"So this means you are in charge now. What is the status of the terrorists?" A third reporter asked.

Jacob kept his concerned diplomatic face on, "All captured terrorists are being questioned. We expect more to be picked up soon, and the military is working hard to ensure no other horrible acts take place."

Another reporter shouted out a question, "Are there enough buildings in each area to house the people who are being moved in? How about large buildings for distribution centers? We've been told that there are not enough buildings to accommodate all of the people let alone enough warehouses large enough to support distribution centers."

"We have a special committee that will hire contractors to fulfill all of the needs we have that are not available," Jacob smiled as if to say the peoples' representatives are on the ball. "The National Guard of each state and our military are working with FEMA in every city that is absorbing new people to ensure temporary sites are set up where there is a shortage so all can be accommodated."

Jacob turned to leave even though the reporters continued to yell out questions. One reporter turned to the camera and spoke to the people.

"Good morning from Statuary Hall. You just heard Speaker Peterson's update. There are many questions still to be answered, and you can be assured we will continue to keep you informed as new information becomes available. As the Speaker said, we all need to pray for those taken hostage and whose fate is unknown at this time. This is Russell signing off from the Capitol."

CHAPTER SEVEN

Gregg watched the briefing from his living room. He knew Peterson was not sincere about his concern for the President or anyone else. After what Jody said the night before and knowing Peterson was anything but troubled, he decided he was going to take matters into his own hands and take control of the situation.

He called Mark, "Anything yet?"

"No, they're just finishing up spraying the place down so there aren't any hot spots. I bet this afternoon they'll start searching," his friend answered.

Gregg was silent. "You still there buddy?" Mark asked.

"Yeah, I'm here. Why don't one of you stay there and the rest come back. I'll need your help getting info out of the Pentagon and FBI. This is the last stage of our country's takeover, so it's time we did something. We've sat around long enough and let those assholes do as they pleased without any accountability, and that is about to end."

"Okay," Mark said a little bewildered, "we'll leave Leo here, and the rest of us will head back. Should be back early this afternoon."

That afternoon, Mark, Max, and Gunman showed up at Gregg's wondering what was coming next. The four sat at the kitchen table and looked at each other.

"We have work to do," Gregg told them. "This isn't over by a long shot, and those bastards are going to be held accountable this time."

Gunman looked at his friend, "You know, Gregg, that guy you showed us a picture of, the FBI guy, he's the one we should be looking for."

Max nodded, "Yeah, just as we thought. He was the leader and was with the guards who went in the building the night before we were set to go in. We should be going after him, because he could answer all of our questions and probably tell things we don't even think to ask."

Mark looked around the table, "Gregg, maybe we're jumping the gun here. Maybe Jamie wasn't there."

"I know," he smiled at his friend. "So we're going to find out and do much more than that. We are going to stop this top-down takeover of our country. I don't give a damn how much money they have. It's time for every citizen in this nation to take a stand, especially the military. We all took oaths to defend the Constitution against foreign and domestic enemies. Looks like we have quite a few domestic enemies."

Mark was surprised at what his buddy said. "He's right," he told the others. "We took that oath too, and it's time we honored it. Gunman talk to everybody you know. Somebody knows something, so get it. Max, you do the same thing. I'll do my research too, and we'll meet back here in two days to decide where we go from here."

Everybody across the nation was on edge to see what had happened to the President and his group and what was going to happen to many citizens who were being moved. Many were wondering why they needed distribution centers for food instead of letting businesses stay open that could obtain food from places not affected by the radiation. Even though thousands of people contacted their senators and representatives in Washington, they didn't receive any answers.

Two days later, Jacob addressed all of the congresspeople and senators who were waiting in the House Chamber. The speech was seen as a relief for some of them so they could answer their constituents' questions. But more officials on Capitol Hill were worried about their own status not what they could tell their people. Their anticipation grew.

Peterson walked to the podium and began his discourse which he hoped would settle many things his peers had been asking about. "We've just received word from the FBI. With sincere regret, I am reporting to you that the President's remains were found in Baltimore. The Vice President was found as well. It is believed that the persons who held the President and his V.P. hostage have been arrested. I am truly sorry to have to bring you this news, and as updates come in, I will let you know. Thank you."

Everyone in the room was in shock because they had not expected to hear what he said. They couldn't understand how something like this could happen with all of the security that is always in place. The secret service would never have let people close enough to those in office for something like this to happen.

Some wondered if a copycat terrorist would start to bomb or try to take hostages. Most of the people in the room started to devise plans on how they could catch the Speaker's attention now that he was next in line for the Presidency. They would jockey for higher level jobs that always came open when a new President took office. This could be their chance to reign over the rest.

Senator Stu Seagly stopped to speak to Jacob quietly. "Jacob, something is very wrong here. We are going to call a committee together to investigate all of this. Have you gotten secret service reports to find out what happened? Someone taking the President and his staff hostage and then killing them is not feasible with the security they had. So many terrorists bombing at one time with no warning from our national security is impossible."

Jacob smiled, "Yes, this must have been planned carefully. We will get the truth as we interrogate the suspects."

"No Jacob," Stu looked him in the eye, "this looks like it was planned from within. I am asking the Pentagon and the FBI to find out immediately who was involved in this. We will discover who the masterminds were, and they will be held accountable." He gave Jacob a look of distrust and moved on.

Lucy came up from behind, "Don't pay any attention to him, Jacob. What can he do? We'll have the presidency, both Houses of Congress, more judges than we'll be able to use, and the media. His committees won't do a thing but waste more time and public money."

"I know, he's just trying to get under my skin to see if I'll blow," Jacob looked at her with a smile. "He won't get to me, but I am getting tired of this whole process. I'm ready to take control and get things done. Come on, I have to get to Statuary Hall to address the nation."

This time only the media stood around waiting to hear what he had to say. Jacob stood up to the microphone and began, "Good morning, everyone. It is with deep regret that I report to you that the President and Vice President have died in the apartment building explosion in Baltimore. There are several suspects who have been arrested and are being interrogated. I can assure each and every one of you that we will find out what happened. As I am next in line, I will be the President until such time as a new president is elected. We will report back to you as more facts are revealed. Thank you."

The media was so stunned it took them a few seconds to even think about asking questions. Peterson didn't care. He turned and walked away without even noticing no questions were flying at him.

In the Longworth Building many congresspeople and senators stopped by Jacob's office all afternoon. Most were dazed and unbelieving of what happened, and many started to worry about themselves. Were there terrorists out there who were also going to target people in Congress? They were also concerned about Peterson's plans to move ahead. The Speaker was inheriting a huge job, and not everyone was certain he was up to the challenge. Running the House was a lot different than managing the country, so they would all have to do what they could to keep the nation moving forward smoothly.

Several senators spoke with Jacob for a while about his plans, and all Jacob could tell them was everyone had to work together and do what was best for the country.

A few miles away in Gregg's living room, he and his friends were meeting. Gregg was angry, "That son-of-a-bitch Peterson didn't even mention the other people who were in that building. Bastard. You know we still haven't gotten official word that Jamie was with them. I'll bet none of the other families have either. They have the obligation to let the next of kin know, so are they just going to forget about them?"

The other guys looked at each other and then back at Gregg.

"Sorry buddy," Gunman was feeling bad for his friend, "but I was told the whole group was in the building when it blew. I know some guys in the secret service, and they know no one got out of there alive. He said they're going to continue going through the rubble until they find everyone who was in there. He also was pretty quiet about the secret service who were protecting them." Gunman and the others knew from experience that the security for the government officials in the building had been pulled.

Leo was back because there wasn't anything for him to do in Baltimore. They could find out as much in D.C. as he could waiting by the explosion site. Leo had done some checking too, "I found out that Randy is Peterson's puppet and was paid by him to make sure they never got out of that building. Can't prove that yet, but we will. In fact, Randy was one of the ones picked up by the FBI a day or so ago and put in jail to be interrogated. I'll bet he's mad as hell. Doing all that work for the government and being put in jail for it."

"Peterson planned the whole thing from the beginning," Mark snapped. "Top of the heap in our government. That figures."

Leo nodded, "Yup, but we have to prove that and find out who else was in on it. Could be just about anybody in that Capitol. Only a few up there are honest. I'll bet once they get mileage out of Randy and his pals, the top layer will have him killed. They have to so they can keep what they did hidden."

Gregg had calmed down, "We don't know who was in that building and who was taken somewhere else. Until I'm told Jamie is gone, she is still alive to me. But we have to get busy now, so Leo and Mark, you both know how to get in the jail to see Randy. Persuade him to talk and get it recorded. If you're right, we have to get that info out of him quickly before anything happens to him."

"I'll find out who else was in on this. It will take some time, but it's doable," Leo told them confidently.

Mark looked around the table, "Just remember that we have to be able to prove everything."

"That's right," Gregg agreed. "I don't care how long this takes. We'll find out what happened."

The guys left and Gregg sat in his living room knowing he had to talk to Jody. Should he tell her what Gunman said? Was Jamie alive or dead? "Well, I'll go over and talk to her."

Jody opened the door when Gregg knocked. "Hi Gregg."

She opened the door wide so he could step in. "Hi Jody," and then he stepped up to her and gave her a big hug. She started crying, so they sat on her couch and she cried until she couldn't cry anymore.

"The bastard never even mentioned Jamie," she looked away as if she was trying to picture where Jamie was.

Gregg held her hand, "I know."

"I can't work for that son-of-a-bitch anymore," Jody began to wipe the tears from her eyes. "I'm going to clean out my desk tomorrow, and I'll find a job somewhere else. He is such a pig!"

"I know what you're feeling, but don't quit yet. My buddies and I are going to find out what happened. We may need your help inside, and we can't be sure about Jamie yet. Those bastards could have taken her somewhere else and not even to that apartment building," Gregg gave her a smile.

"Who would do this?" Jodie asked blowing her nose. "What's the purpose or point of this whole thing?"

"It's all for power, Jody. It certainly is an inside job, and we're going to prove who was involved. It may take a long time to do that, but I'm not going to give up until I know where Jamie is and who did this to her," Gregg started to get angry again.

Jody wiped her nose again, "Well there's a whole bunch of assholes up there who only care about themselves. How much power do they need? Most of them are rich from selling us out, so do they have to destroy the country too?"

"You're right on point. I don't know when it will be enough for any of them, but I do know that sooner or later they will get what they deserve." Gregg turned to his sister-in-law with a kind smile that said everything would be alright.

He got back to his house and was exhausted from all of the emotions that had been flowing for days. He took his wallet out of his back pocket and laid it on the table by the bed. Unbuttoning his shirt, he headed for the shower. He had just turned on the water when a knock came on the front door. "Who in the hell can that be?"

Putting his shirt back on, he opened the door and saw a man who was holding an FBI badge. Gregg said nothing but stared at the person. The FBI agent began the conversation, "I'm certain you are already aware that your wife was on the list of people who were with the President in Baltimore. We haven't been able to identify anyone but the President and Vice President so far. Most of the rest of the group with the President were in different rooms, and there were a number of residents who were also in the building. As soon as we positively identify anyone, we are immediately letting their family know."

Gregg just continued to look at the man without saying a word and without showing any emotion.

"I am sorry this is taking so long, but please believe we are working as quickly as we can," the FBI agent looked at Gregg with sympathy and kindness. "Goodnight, sir."

The day came for the final service at the Church to lay the President and Vice President to rest. Days before a huge procession with marching bands and a horse with boots turned backwards in the saddle's stirrups intensified the beginning of saying farewell to the leaders of the country. The President's body was carried by the funeral carriage while an honor guard marched in step beside it. The Vice President's coffin followed with an identical honor guard. The streets were lined with spectators watching the great, historical event. Both had lain in the Rotunda once they had reached the Capitol, and those who wished to pass by silently to pay their respects had the opportunity. Finally, it was the day for the funerals of the President and Vice President. It was thought by the families that it would be better to have a double funeral to help give the country completeness and closure.

Jacob had moved in to the oval office, and on the day of the funeral he was in that office talking to Richard, an FBI agent. Richard was telling the new President all of the details of what had occurred with the terrorists up to that point.

Richard also brought a request to Jacob, "One of the people picked up for the hotel bombing insists he needs to talk to you. His name is Randy, and he tells us you hired him and another detained terrorist to find enough people to plan the attack with the dirty bombs."

Jacob was indignant "They will say anything to take the focus off of themselves. I want those two gone by the end of the day. Maybe one of their buddies got some cyanide pills through to them."

Richard was shocked, "Sir, I can't ….."

"Shut up!" Jacob said quickly. "Done by the end of today or you might find charges against yourself by the end of the day. And I don't want any of this released to the public. We'll continue to handle the terrorists through the court system, and those two will just disappear quietly. I'm tired of people thinking they can come up against this government and win. Every time any of them speak their mind against us, they will suffer hard consequences."

Richard left the oval office and went to FBI Headquarters. He walked into his supervisor's office and laid his badge on the desk telling his superior he was through. His boss tried to talk to him, "You'll lose all of your years of service which means your pension. Are you crazy? What happened? Let's talk about it."

"I can't work with this President. I won't do what he wants done, and I'm not willing to go to jail because I didn't do what he wanted. He's a lunatic, and I won't work for his Administration," Richard was firm and walked out of the office.

His boss sat looking out of the window. He knew he would have to find out what the President wanted and ensure it was done or he would lose his job. He wondered what it could possibly be.

Reaching over to his phone, he called the White House and asked the President's secretary for a meeting that day. Jody told him that the President was just about to leave for the funerals, and he would not be available until four o'clock. The FBI supervisor said he would be there then.

People were gathered all around the National Cathedral that afternoon. Some were praying, some were crying, and some were protesting the changes that had taken place in society. A news reporter was talking to the nation showing those interested what was going on outside of the Church before the service. He decided to ask people what they thought about the situation in the country.

"Hello sir, can you tell me what you think of the situation our country finds itself in?"

The man turned to the reporter, "We definitely were attacked by terrorists. I can't believe this is happening. They said the people who detonated the bombs were from Asia, so maybe we shouldn't just let anyone into our country. Perhaps we should investigate people before they come in."

"How about you sir," the reporter asked another man. "Where do you think our country is headed?"

"Well, I think we all need to follow the direction we are given by our government. None of us needs to be around radiation. We're definitely stumbling at the moment, but we'll come around and fix all of this," he said looking at the camera.

The reporter decided to get the viewpoint of one more person, "How about you? What do you think of how our government is handling things?"

This time he asked a woman, and she turned to look at who was speaking to her then at the camera, "I think this was all planned by our government. They are scaring the public so badly the Administration can do anything it wants, and no one is asking why. I don't trust anything that is going on right now, and I hope the people stand against all of the changes that are taking place and the freedoms that are being taken away."

The reporter went back by the front door of the Cathedral to make certain the public saw who was attending the funeral. Many congresspeople and senators were brought up to the front of the Church and dropped off by their chauffeurs. There were multiple diplomats in town on business who attended, and quite a few business executives were also seen.

Finally, Jacob was seen getting out of his limousine, 'The Beast', and entering the Church. Some people on the street tried to enter the Cathedral after him, and they were turned away. They squinted their eyes before they left the steps trying to see into the dim Church.

The media inside did their best to show the public how beautiful the Cathedral looked that day. Not only were there beautiful flowers on the altar, but all different types and different colors were placed around the Church sending off a sweet, beautiful smell. Each pew had a bouquet attached to each end, and there was also a stunning arrangement by the podium.

Guests filled the building, and many prominent people had come to say goodbye to the nation's Executives. Speakers for the day included one of the sons of the deceased President, the daughter of the late Vice President, the new Speaker of the House, the Senate Majority Leader, and President Peterson.

Peterson was the last to speak. He stood at the podium and began his speech, and by the time he had finished, people were amazed at the end of his discourse. "Our late President worked, as past presidents have done, to continuously change our nation for the better. He helped set the stage for huge transformation, and I intend to continue his work. We will all miss the people who guided our nation these last three years, but I can assure you I will work very hard to improve our nation's health and prosperity."

Once Peterson was back in the Oval Office, his secretary told him that he had a visitor from the FBI. Jacob told her to send him in.

"Hello sir, I'm Jeff, a supervisor at the FBI. One of my team members, Richard, quit today, and he did tell me that there was something you wanted him to do. As Richard is no longer able to fulfill your request, I am here to see what I can do for you, sir."

Jacob looked annoyed and told the man he would accomplish the task another way. "I appreciate your coming here, but any further action on your part is unnecessary."

"Thank you, sir, and if you decide you do need the FBI to complete a mission, please let us know." Jeff smiled and then left the Oval Office wondering what it could have been that made his employee decide to quit.

Jacob knew Jeff was in a high-level FBI job, but he decided he would go even higher to ensure this task was taken care of. "Jody, please get the Chairman of the Joint Chiefs on the phone."

Jody made the call and had the Chairman on the line. "Hi Dick," Jacob greeted his old friend. "Could you come over this afternoon? There's an operation that I would like you to oversee and ensure that it is taken care of."

That afternoon, Dick was in Peterson's office, "Hi Jacob. What is it that I can assist with?"

Jacob closed the door of his office and told Dick what needed to be done under complete secrecy. He gave the names of the two that needed to be taken care of and the emphasis was that it should not be reported to the public.

"Wouldn't the FBI be a better source for this?" Dick asked.

"I already went to the FBI, and they were a disappointment on this issue. Instead of going higher there, I am putting it in your hands to ensure a special ops person takes care of it with little problem. Part of your duties now include terrorists within our borders."

"Right," Dick agreed. "It will be accomplished by nightfall sir." Dick left, and Jacob continued on with the plans he was making for the next time he addressed the nation.

CHAPTER EIGHT

Max and Gunman went to Gregg's, and the three sat around waiting for Mark and Leo to get back from the jail. Gunman got up and looked out the window, "What are we going to do with these guys if Mark and Leo can get them recorded? We can't protect them."

"They won't tell our guys who the masterminds were while they're still in jail. They'll use that to make us get them out. They might tell us if they took Jamie somewhere else and maybe give us some names of those who worked with them, but they won't mention Peterson. So we're going to wait until they get out and then make them tell us who gave the order to light the bombs. They're going to help us get rid of the ones who planned this," Max smiled at his buddy.

Hours later, Leo and Mark walked through the door. "The son-of-a-bitch had him killed. Yeah, we got into the jail through a contact to talk to Randy. Before we could get to his cell, a guard stopped us and told us to turn around," Leo told the group.

Mark nodded, "We went back and waited at the front desk, and our guy comes out and says Randy and his buddy killed themselves. They didn't tell us how."

Leo added, "They didn't kill themselves. They were murdered, and we'll find out how as soon as the autopsies are done."

Gregg let out a big sigh and started tapping on the table. A minute later he told them, "Give me some time to figure out what we're going to do next. This isn't over." His friends knew Gregg would come up with something.

A couple days later, Jacob was getting ready to address the country from the East Room of the White House. Everyone at the Capitol was waiting in the House Chamber for him to appear on TV, and as they waited, several in Congress discussed the things that were being done. They weren't happy with the way things were being handled, but the majority followed along so they could keep in Jacob's good graces.

Senator Stu Seagly was one who disagreed, and he was talking to a group of congressmen and senators in the Chamber as they waited for Jacob.

Anna

"Did you see the directives Jacob is going to give to the public this time? This is all hogwash, and he's pushing his power grab too far. When the bills come up for a vote, we have to vote them down."

Some who listened to Seagly agreed, and then they stopped talking as Jacob came on the screen. Peterson wanted to ensure his power was solid, and he knew he had to keep the people obeying his directions. Stepping up to the podium, he laid his briefing folder on the stand. He glanced around the room at the media. They were prepared and ready to broadcast the update across all of their channels so the entire nation could see it.

"Good afternoon. We have updated information concerning the attacks we went through. Although it has taken some time, we now have accurate data on the radiation that was released throughout our country. Multiple sites across the nation have been tested, and it has been found that the radiation emitted from the bombs was the deadliest and most long-lasting type that can be found outside of what the atomic bomb generates. We will continue to measure the radioactivity in the contaminated areas, but returning to the affected regions will not happen for a very long time.

Our government is taking great action to ensure our lives can go on while making certain we are safe. The number of permanent distribution centers in existing buildings is growing rapidly, and soon the temporary sites will be disbanded. In rural areas where people cannot walk to their centers, trucks are supplying citizens' needs by utilizing a firm schedule. In this way, we know the items people are receiving have not been contaminated.

Due to all businesses being closed, obtaining all medical prescriptions and visiting a medical professional will be done through the distribution centers. Everyone will go to the allocation places to acquire what they need from this point forward. Those in rural areas will need to let personnel on the distribution trucks know what they require, and personnel will ensure medicine and care is available.

As you know, many existing buildings are being or have been renovated to permanent classrooms and dormitories. For the sites that have been completed, it is now time for the children between five and eighteen to move into these dormitories. This movement will continue in each area as soon as new sites are ready. All children will be checked for radiation, so parents will not have to worry about their children being exposed to any danger.

Where there are not suitable sites, construction will begin. As there is no more need for private ownership, the existing sites being put to use and the new construction sites will become the property of the government. The Administration will have to take possession of this land to be able to build or use existing structures where it is necessary to serve all of our people for current and future needs.

As all of these actions are being accomplished to benefit the public, the expense to achieve all of this will be enormous. Due to the closing of all non-government businesses and services, we are going to use our technology to benefit everyone. All financial and asset transactions will be accomplished and tracked electronically. We will use digital money for all of our needs, and hard currency will no longer be utilized. Paper documents will cease to exist with this new process.

The government must be able to afford to feed and clothe all of our citizens, provide medication, provide medical care, move those from the contaminated areas, and continue educating our children. Because of the needs of all of our people, our situation requires that each household work with government to make this possible. The Internal Revenue Service, or IRS, will be electronically transferring all accounts of money and financial assets our people have in banks, credit unions, and any other holder of money, bonds, IRAs, CDs, stocks, etc. to the government. The Administration will utilize these assets to take care of our people. All other assets such as vehicles, equipment, precious metals, commodities, etc. will be moved over to government ownership as well. We are placing many more people into IRS positions, and these new agents will be out in the field very soon to accomplish this.

As your government is going to take complete care of each and every one of you, all assistance programs will stop immediately. This includes Social Security, Medicare, Medicaid, Bridge Cards, and all other types of assistance. Please understand that we are in a crisis situation, and we must deal with it in a way that will serve all.

Anna

Our country needs your support during this time of catastrophe. We must be able to rebuild our nation and take care of ourselves with the assistance of our allies. Because our nation needs a solid foundation to accomplish this, every adult person who is able must help our country survive. So, each person will be given a job from the government, or the government will decide if a person cannot work. Whether the job is in a factory, office building, or outside in the environment, the job given will remain that person's for the rest of their life so they can earn a living. The government will issue cards allotting each person credit per month for working, and through this process, people can use their credit to purchase what they need at the distribution centers.

I understand these changes are huge. We are setting up a Distribution Agency that can answer your questions, give job assignments, check people for ability to work, and also distribute allotment cards. We know that this has never been done before, but it is urgent that we all work together to provide what our country requires.

As President, I have used Executive Orders to make these acts law to assist our population as quickly as possible. I know that each and every one of you are true patriots and see that the avenues being taken will allow us to achieve the most at this juncture in our nation's history. This will allow us to continue our democracy in our great nation. Thank you for all of your support as we work tirelessly to serve you."

Jacob stepped away from the podium and looked at the media. No one said a word, but mouths were opened and eyes were searching the room looking to others for an explanation of what just happened. Peterson left the room and went directly back to the Oval Office.

Not a person watching the update in the House Chamber could believe what they heard. They all knew that this was the final stage to move the country to a non-democratic nation with a dictator at the top. They were going over the available options in their minds. Follow Jacob and maybe succeed, or go against Jacob and be thrown in prison. They knew a decision would have to be made by each one very soon.

Once in his office, Jacob poured himself a drink to try and calm his nerves. He wondered if the people would riot after what he just said.

82

Lucy got to the White House and went directly to his office. "You really had the guts to do it. I'll bet very few citizens resist, so we should be home free. If a few do come out against us, we'll just throw them in jail and call them terrorists. That will squelch any larger protests. Wow, all of the years spent confusing people by the ridiculous rules we pushed out to the media worked like a charm. Burning anything in sight and encouraging riots was calm protesting, telling the people they weren't women or men but nonbinary, making people feel ashamed if they put children's welfare over a male who said he was a woman, and on and on has paid off. There isn't even any radiation, but no one asked to see the reports, and even if they did we could push them off and ignore them. People who test those things just thought someone else took samples and determined the potency of the fallout. No one knows what is right or wrong anymore, so very few will take a stand against anything we do," she laughed with delight. "We have intimidated almost everyone!"

Jacob smiled, "I'm not done yet. Because we are running everything, we are going to have to do something about too much population. The people will have on-demand abortions, but there may still be more people than what we need to do the work with all of the immigrants being made citizens."

"What's your plan?" Lucy asked concerned.

"Well," Jacob smiled, "when kids are five, they go to the government school camps. So, when some of them are between seven and twelve, the excess will be sold to countries that use slaves."

Lucy looked at him, "What countries? Oh, China, India, Libya and those that still buy and use slaves. That will bring in billions of dollars if we do that right."

"And maybe we can talk other countries that currently don't use slave labor into using people this way. The more the better because most of that money will go into my pocket!" Jacob exclaimed.

"Let's not forget about our senior citizens," he was considering options. "We'll have to make rules about who gets medicine because the supply will be low. Too low for maybe those over sixty to get any unless, of course, they are the chosen politicians or the rich. That will reduce the population from the bottom and top leaving the most physically able middle layer to do the work that needs to be done and using fewer resources to keep them. That will make life much nicer for the special people like us.

We are also going to slowly get rid of the troublemakers by increasing the availability of free drugs. Many of those who didn't learn a thing in the last generation but spent their time stealing, burning, injuring and killing people will die from drug overdose. Those who don't die will go to the labor camps to work hard the rest of their lives. No more crime or problems. How's that for reparation? They did their job of producing unrest and crime when it was needed, but now we want calm and routine, so they will be taken care of. The closer we get to running like a communist regime, the better off everything will be."

"Brilliant," Lucy laughed clinking her glass with his.

People started rioting and protesting all over D.C. Even some governors were trying to fight back against the ridiculous laws Jacob was enacting. As soon as the protests began, the military was there to take the people away. They were put in jail and transferred to a rebel camp where they would remain until Peterson decided to let them go. He wanted people to know they would be jailed so protests would stop. This was his country now, and he would do anything necessary to stop rebellious activity and put people in their place.

The next day Jody waited for Jacob to leave his office. Once she knew he was in a meeting for most of the afternoon, she went in and took the recorder hidden behind a book by the door. She knew this was probably the only way to get news about Jamie and the others who disappeared but had been forgotten. The FBI still had no answers for any of those who were with the President. She chose the spot behind the book because it was out of the camera's range. If she was caught, she would be fired and sent to prison for sure. The thought of those things happening didn't faze her, because she was too worried about Jamie. In her mind her sister was still alive. The recorder might give her at least clues to let her know Jamie was alright and maybe where she was.

After she got home from work that afternoon, Jody sat in her living room with the recorder in her hand. "I can't believe the speech he gave yesterday. I hope people don't just do what they are told by a tyrant who doesn't care about anyone but himself. He'll keep taking things away until there is nothing left to take and he has control of it all."

She started the recorder and heard all that Jacob said to Lucy the afternoon before. Jody was astounded that he was that bold and corrupt, and she knew she wasn't going to let him get away with it.

Dialing Gregg's number, she looked out of the window and angrily thought of how some people could care so little about their country and their fellow citizens. He couldn't have a heart, and probably his soul was owned by the devil. When Gregg answered, Jody began, "Did you hear the speech that bastard gave yesterday?"

"Yes," Gregg sounded angry too. "It was a bunch of bullshit, and I don't think people will put up with it for long."

"I think they will," Jody retorted. "Most people are afraid of the radiation. Some want to complain, but they have no leader and they're afraid they'll just be put in jail. In small numbers we can't do anything, and that bastard knows it. I haven't seen any reports on the radiation, and now I know why. He just wanted to scare people into letting him proceed with his plan to take everything away from everybody. Hey, I want you to listen to this." Jody hit the play button on the recorder, and Gregg listened patiently on the other end. When the conversation was over, she shut it off, "Well, what do you think about that?"

Gregg couldn't believe she had that type of evidence, "How did you get that?"

"I'll tell you when we aren't on the phone," she responded. "I'm going to get more."

"Be careful, Jody," Gregg was amazed. "They don't care who they hurt or kill, so please don't let them find out you're recording them. No radiation at all, and he's moved millions of people, disrupted every life, taken all wealth, and taken away everyone's ability to earn income except what he chooses to give. That son-of-a-bitch is going to sell our kids and kill our seniors! I wonder how many people on the Hill know about this, and how many of them he'll get rid of once he has everything he wants? Look, you better give me that tape. I can let other people know what is going on too, and that may help us knock this bastard off of his throne."

Jody was emphatic, "NO! You can't tell anyone that I recorded them. I'll go to prison for the rest of my life or be sold to China. We don't know who we can trust and who we can't. Anyway, it's not time for that yet. I have to keep recording so we can find out what their next dirty moves are going to be."

"You're right," Gregg agreed. "I'll keep that to myself until there comes a time when you can't be hurt but he can be. Did you leave another recorder to get more information?"

Jody told him she had, and she intended to keep doing it.

"Okay, but make sure the tape you have can't be erased. We'll collect these for the future. Jody, you do know he killed the two men who could identify him as the mastermind of the bombings. Haven't found out how they were killed yet."

"Well, that tells us he'll do anything to keep his power, so be careful Gregg," she told him hoping he wouldn't get hurt either. "We just have to work together and be careful. If we screw up, they'll get away with everything including Jamie."

A few weeks went by, and restorations and construction for the schools and dormitories moved ahead quickly. Many schools had begun teaching, and the dormitories that were ready were full of students. As children were taken from their homes by the military, the parents and any person over eighteen in each household were given a letter to report to the Distribution Agency for a job assignment. Some people in their forties, fifties, and older had never worked or had to decide what to buy from what they earned. They had no experience in managing limited funds for food, clothing, or any other need that must be met. Many of these people complained, but no one who could remedy the matter listened.

Distribution centers were put up in a week or so and ready to go. Unfortunately, more often than not there was a very poor selection of food available. Rarely could people buy meat, vegetables, and fruits at the same time. Often, people would go to the center on their appointed day only to find the shelves were bare.

Clothing was also hard to find in many sizes. Garments were either shipped in from other countries or made within, but production and receipt of shipments could not keep up with the demand for all of the citizens. Shoes became scarce as well, and many had to wear footwear with holes. Complaints rose up to the top levels of government, but the grumbling had no effect on changing the processes to receive greater quantities more often. In fact, those in office never mentioned anything about sympathy for the people. No one in any political party tried to change it.

Of course, the people knew that when it was election time they would vote out the scoundrels who were in office. Unfortunately, they never got the chance. Peterson signed another Executive Order claiming the disaster that hit was still in full force. Because of the radiation, it was not safe for people to leave their homes to vote or open the polling places where ballots could be counted. Voting was suspended until such time that the radioactivity had subsided enough that the nation's environment was safe again.

People complained everywhere, but little could be done to go back to their previous lives. Most of the media called anyone who didn't believe in the new laws terrorists or insurrectionists. As those on TV and the radio continued to berate citizens constantly, those who did dare to complain were picked up and put in jail and eventually sent to a camp. The people had completely lost their sense of a democratic government and freedom. They were letting those in office lead them anywhere the politicians wanted, even to the citizens detriment.

In the Oval Office, Dick, the Chairman of the Joint Chiefs of Staff, stood by the President's desk not accepting the seat that was offered to him. They were discussing the condition of the country. "Sir," Dick offered, "we have been finding issues with martial law and the distribution of food and medicine."

Jacob listened and asked, "Are protesters giving the National Guard and Army problems?"

"No sir," Dick answered, "residents of multiple cities have surrounded their towns and are armed. They refuse to let their children leave, and they will not let the military in to ensure law and order."

"Our military was told to confiscate all of the guns when we moved people out of the radiation areas," Jacob was surprised that hadn't happened. "I also thought that the towns that were taking care of themselves had been dismantled during the moves to new areas."

"Well, sir, the citizens in the bombed areas were moved, but they hid their firearms and went back to get them later. They are working with the townspeople of the new places and are functioning on their own. They take nothing from the distribution centers, so they grow their own food, make their own clothes, do their own building, teach their kids and so forth."

Jacob sat straight up in his chair, "Have any of our military been shot at?"

"Not that I am aware of sir," the Chairman decided to take the offered seat, "but the military has not insisted. They are afraid that if they do, the citizens of these towns will defend themselves to their death."

Jacob looked down at his desk, "How many towns are doing this? I thought this problem had been solved."

Dick shook his head, "I'm sorry to report that's not the case. I know of twenty-five or thirty towns doing this. If those who lived on their own before the bombings can't get the entire town to stand with them, then they take a section of it and blockade it off. Most of the towns have gone along with them, so we are talking about many thousands of people. We are afraid with all the changes being made that many more cities and towns will join them, and then we will have millions of militants on our hands."

Jacob slammed his fist on the desk and stood up, "I want the National Guard and Army to surround these towns and not let anything in. Don't let citizens leave or return. Those bastards are going to learn to submit one way or the other."

"Yes, sir. What of the governors? A few have been objecting and telling their people to resist," Dick looked as though he knew a civil war was ahead.

"Any governor who does not follow my Executive Orders will be arrested," Jacob looked Dick in the eye. "I don't have time to fool around with these punk shits."

"It is possible the National Guard will follow the orders of the governor of their state," the Chairman was trying to put the entire picture in front of Jacob.

"Then any Service or National Guard soldier who does not follow my orders will be thrown in jail and treated as a traitor," Peterson was firm.

"Yes sir," the Chairman saluted and left the room.

Jacob stood up and looked out the window, "Who are these bastards to defy me? They will find out soon enough that their democratic world is over, and they will submit and acknowledge that I am their leader. If they don't, things will get very ugly for them."

He sat back down at his desk and turned the TV on to see what was going on out in the world. A news reporter was interviewing residents from some of the same towns he was just discussing with the Chairman, so he turned the volume up to see what was being said.

The reporter held the microphone up to the first resident, "Sir, can you tell me why the citizens have encircled the town?"

"Those bastards aren't coming in here. They made us move, but we won't be taken over here either. We'll protect our own town and its people. There's no way they're taking our kids. You can tell that asshole who's playing President to go to hell," the man responded.

The reporter moved on, "Ma'am, can you tell me how you will get food for the residents.

She smiled, "We'll bring our own food in or grow it ourselves."

"What will you do about medicine and a process to buy things?" he smiled back at the woman.

"We'll take care of ourselves, and we can always barter," she turned back to the work she was doing before the newsperson stopped her.

He turned to the camera, "There you have it folks. People are forming their own governments and disregarding our federal policy. We'll keep you updated on how these self-sufficient towns are getting along. Have a nice day everyone."

Jacob flicked the TV off and grabbed his phone. Lucy answered and Jacob sputtered, "Did you see the news? Did you see the son-of-a-bitches who are guarding their own towns and not letting the military in? I thought we got rid of those with the bombings. Well, we will get rid of them, and it will be sooner not later."

Lucy talked calmly to try and get Jacob to relax a bit. "I just heard about it. What will we do now?"

Jacob paused, "Look, I'll see you tonight at our usual place. This will get figured out." He hung up and slowly started thinking instead of lashing out.

The next day, Jacob left his office and ran into senators who were waiting to see him.

Stu Seagly was there, "Jacob, this has gone too far. Did you see the news today? Your last speech was so preposterous some of the media can't believe it, and they normally report in our favor. You know what I've always heard is true. When government has a party majority, it becomes tyrannical. This isn't going to go unanswered, Jacob. We will stop you."

Jacob turned to him and said sarcastically, "Go to hell. We have the majority in both Houses, and you can't stop anything."

CHAPTER NINE

Citizens were afraid across the country. Many believed the government, but just as many did not. More and more depression gripped the nation. Fights broke out at the distribution centers with people trying to take more than they were supposed to have. The security guards took some of those away who were grabbing extra, but there were too many. What was left was often not enough for those who still waited in line.

People stood around trying to figure out what was really going on. Some were crying while they waited extended periods for the items they came for. Everyone seemed tired and irritable, and those waiting after a long day at work found it almost unbearable.

A news reporter approached a few people in line. His cameraman was filming as he spoke to them. "Good afternoon, ma'am," the reporter smiled. "Have you been able to obtain the things you need from the center since it has been open?"

"Not really," she answered. "The last time we were here we were given enough for about three days. We couldn't come back for four days because of all the people who have to use this site."

The reporter asked, "So, your biggest concern is not receiving enough food?"

She looked sad, "My biggest concern is that my husband was given a job at this distribution center. I'm afraid there will be trouble and he'll be hurt."

The reporter saw a man standing nearby listening and nodding, "What about you, sir, are all of your needs being met?"

The man stared at the reporter, "Hell no. Half of the food they've got is rotten. No medicine today at all. I'm going to try another site tomorrow to see if I can get what I need. My boy has to have his pills or he will die, but those bastards here in D.C. don't care about that."

The reporter looked at the camera, "This site is definitely having problems providing for the people. Several other sites we visited were doing fine, so maybe it is just a matter of learning what works and what doesn't. Signing off from the distribution center on Fifth Street. Have a nice day folks."

91

Several blocks away, the guys met back at Gregg's house. Leo asked the others, "Have any of you been to one of those distribution places yet?"

The others shook their heads no, and Leo continued, "Damn, you can't get much there. I heard people in some areas are starving because the food they got was rotten or getting that way. Not much of a selection at all in other areas, and many of those places run out completely."

"Yeah, it was in the news today," Max agreed. "The government is supposed to be bringing in lots more food in a couple of days so people don't revolt. But medicine is not available lots of places and not just in a few like the people in D.C. want us to think. The military taking the kids is a big issue that I don't think is going to go away. I got my news on line at a site the government hasn't taken over yet."

Gunman had seen this all before, "They'll figure out just how much has to be available to keep the people quiet. Seen some of this at one of the places I was stationed. The dictators give just enough, and the people just take it. And they'll keep taking it until the tyrants make a mistake and take too much away. Then the shit hits the fan."

"That will definitely happen the way Peterson is going," Mark said. "It's just a matter of time, but I don't understand people just taking this crap without a word. I know they're afraid they'll go to jail, but hell if enough people got together Peterson and his group would have to listen."

"Hey, did you guys find out what happened to Randy and the other guy?" Gregg asked.

"Should find out tomorrow," Leo answered. "What are we going to do then?"

"We've got Peterson's crony on tape saying there was no radiation fallout from the bombs. That was a scam on every American. So, we get all the information we have together and take it to the law asking for Peterson and the others to be charged for all they've done," Gregg said.

Right then, Leo's phone vibrated and slowly moved across the table. He answered it, "Yeah. What?" He looked around at his buddies, "Help us God Almighty! The distribution center on Thirteenth Street was just blown up! Shit, look at these pictures my friend sent."

They all looked at Leo's phone and saw a building that was completely blown apart. Fires were everywhere, and the people they saw were covered with soot and debris. Gregg turned the TV on quickly, and a newscaster was on the scene almost immediately. The camera and microphone were set up in seconds, and the newscaster began.

"As you can see behind me, one of the distribution sites has been blown apart. We haven't received word yet on whether this was an attack or an accident. People are streaming out of the center. The first responders are just getting here, and the police have blocked off the area. We have no way of knowing how many fatalities or injuries there are. Here comes a man who was inside during the explosion. Sir, can you tell us what happened?"

The man was holding a rag to his head. Blood was oozing down his cheek, and there were lacerations on his face, neck, and hands that were deep and wide. "I don't know what happened. It might have been an accident because they were making some food with propane grills. There were quite a few people in there when the thing exploded. I don't see many out here." The man moved on towards the first responders for assistance.

The newscaster saw a woman walking toward her who was crying, "Ma'am, did you see what happened?"

The lady wiped her tear stained cheeks with the back of her hand, "No. All I know is that the person next to me was blown off his feet. My daughter is still in there! I can't find her! I need to find her!"

The newscaster put her hand on the woman's shoulder, "Let the experts find her, ma'am. I'm sure she will be alright." Turning back to the camera she said, "Signing off at the Thirteenth Street center."

Gunman's phone started ringing, so he answered it. "Hey Chet, what's up?"

"I'm by the distribution center that just blew up," his friend was talking very fast. "I saw some regular looking civilians running from the center."

Gunman looked confused, "Why would they blow up their own people and the things they're trying to get at the center?"

"You're right," Chet looked towards the area where the people ran. "Let me track them. I'll find out who they are."

Gunman clicked off his phone, "I've got guys watching."

"That's exactly what we're going to have to do," Gregg smiled at Gunman. "Either I'm really wrong, or the people who blew that place up were told to do it. They're sending a message to the people to stop complaining or they won't have any food at all."

Leo looked at his phone, "Just got a text. That Randy and his buddy took cyanide pills. Believe that? Do they have those in stock at prisons?"

Gunman looked at Gregg, "Who are you planning to turn the information we have over to?"

Max shook his head, "That might be a mistake. If we try to do that, we'll all have a target on our back."

"We have to try. Gregg's right," Mark looked at the others.

"Jody said Senator Stu Seagly disagrees with everything Peterson does," Gregg took one of the recorders out of his pocket. "I'll have her make an appointment with Seagly and see what he says about the damning information we have. I'm going by myself so you guys won't be involved and won't be in danger. I'll see what he's got to say, and we'll know where to go from there."

Gregg called Jody and asked her to make an appointment for him with Seagly. She agreed and called one of his staffers to set up the appointment. Then Jody called Gregg back, "Hi Gregg. Your appointment with Seagly is at ten tomorrow morning. I told his staffer it was about Jamie."

"Thanks Jody," Gregg smiled as he hung up the phone. He felt good about this and was pretty sure the Senator would help them get this information out to the public. After that, he believed it would be fairly simple to get people involved in breaking up the dictatorship that had slithered quietly into control.

The next morning, Gregg got to Stu's office and walked in. He introduced himself to the receptionist and sat in a chair waiting to be called. Looking around the exterior office, he was surprised to see a picture of Seagly, Jacob, and others from Congress together at an outing and acting like they were best friends. There was also an achievement plaque from Stu's hometown supporters and a thank you letter from a woman he had helped among the other special acknowledgements that hung on the wall.

As he gazed around, the Senator came out and stuck his hand out in welcome. He asked Gregg to follow him into his office, and they both took a seat. The Senator started, "I was told this meeting is about your wife Jamie."

"Yes," Gregg said, "partly. Jamie hasn't been found yet, and she was supposedly with the group in the Baltimore hotel."

The Senator smiled at his guest, "I know that it is taking quite a long time for the experts to go through everything. Please be patient, and you will have news as soon as possible."

Gregg took one of the recorders out of his pocket. "Yeah, that's what I've been told. There's another reason I wanted to speak to you. I have recordings and documentation that point to Peterson as the one who hired the people to detonate the bombs and then had them killed. I've also got evidence that there was no radiation in the bombs, and Peterson and his coconspirators are planning to sell some of our kids from the government campuses."

Both men sat there and stared at each other. Stu was no longer smiling, and neither one knew what the other was thinking. Finally, the Senator spoke very quietly. "How did you get this information?"

"That I can't tell you," Gregg said looking directly into the Senator's eyes. "It's solid evidence of actions taken by government officials directly against our citizens. I have recordings and messages."

Stu kept tapping a pencil on the top of his desk, "Did Jacob or any of the others know you were recording them?"

"No," Gregg responded without being intimidated. "If he had known, he wouldn't have said what he did. Isn't that how politicians work?"

The Senator looked at Gregg with understanding, "Look Gregg, I appreciate the fact that you are upset with what has happened. Everyone is, and not everyone agrees with Peterson. But I have to warn you that you can get into big trouble if you try to submit evidence that may be against the law because of the way you obtained it. I'm certain you know government officials are not friendly if someone tries to accuse them of something."

"You don't even want to listen to what was recorded or read the messages?" Gregg asked disappointed.

The Senator shook his head no.

Gregg fully understood where he stood at that moment in time, "So, government officials can break the law and nothing can be done about it?"

"Any type of accusation against an elected official is very hard to prove," Stu looked convinced. "I've seen many politicians accused of wrong doing and they always have a classified reason for their actions, or it wasn't them, or some other excuse. And if the allegations are investigated, ninety-nine percent of the time they are dropped. After that, the person making the claim is seen as an enemy and pursued by the official. Many times the person making the complaint has their life ruined because they were patriotic."

"And you go along with that?" Gregg was plainly disgusted. "You won't help our people or try to stop this tyranny?"

"Look, I'm trying to do things in my official capacity. I know there is a lot wrong here, but it has to be done the right way or change will never happen," Stu said regretfully. "Right now, it is bad timing to try to amend anything. It's very hard for any of us to even try to talk to him. You might want to make absolute certain with a lawyer that the evidence you have was obtained within the law and can be used in a viable accusation."

Gregg stood and looked at yet another politician who didn't give a damn. "Thank you for your time, Senator." He didn't shake the hand that was offered to him but turned and walked out the door without another word.

Stu sat and watched him leave thinking to himself, "I'm afraid there are many Greggs out there, and I don't know how far Jacob can push them. There should be something that can be done, but I'm not sure what that is. D.C. has gone too far this time, and I don't know if the politicians can survive this."

After Gregg got home, he paced back and forth. Where could they go from here. A knock came at the door, and Leo and Mark were standing there. Gregg was glad to see them, "Come on in."

"What happened?" Leo asked anxiously.

Gregg shook his head, "Not much. He warned me not to turn in a complaint until I talk to a lawyer and make sure we can use the information we have. I don't think anyone on the Hill would help us no matter what. From our meeting, I know he and most politicians are afraid of Jacob. The Senator doesn't like what Peterson is doing, but he really didn't say he had a plan to stop all of this. To me, it looks like Peterson has a clear way ahead for the top tyrant job."

"What about Oscar," Mark offered. "He was a lawyer in the military, and I think he still works with the military."

Leo smiled, "He did get us out of a lot of trouble. Isn't he in San Francisco, or maybe he's in San Diego."

"I'm not sure," Gregg took the recorder out of his pocket and laid it on the table. "Gunman will know though."

A little later, Max and Gunman got to Gregg's. Gunman laid some papers on the table and went to get a beer out of the refrigerator.

"What's this?" Gregg picked up one of the pages to look at it.

Gunman took a swig of beer and sat the bottle on the table, "These are pictures of the guys who blew up that distribution center. See anything that looks familiar?"

Everyone looked at the pictures to see if they recognized the men or anything else in the photos.

Leo started to stare at one particular photo. "Wait a minute! This one has a patch on his sleeve like Randy had on his in that picture Jody sent. Some kind of symbol, but I don't know what it means."

"Yeah, that's their gang symbol," Gunman took another drink. "So we know at least this one guy that blew up the distribution center is from the same bunch that did the bombs."

Gregg laid the pictures he held back on the table, "Gunman, do you know where Oscar is?"

"Yeah, why?" Gunman stacked the pictures back into a pile.

Gregg smiled at his buddy, "That Senator I talked to thinks we should check with a lawyer before filing a complaint about Peterson."

"I've got his number," Gunman took his phone out and tapped on Oscar's name.

"Hello," Oscar answered the phone.

"Hey Oscar, it's Gunman. Gregg wants to talk to you." Gunman handed the phone over.

"Hi Oscar," Gregg started to pace again. "How are you doing? Listen, we have recordings of the guy who planned the bombings around the country. Are they admissible in court?"

"Did he know he was being recorded?" Oscar asked.

"No," Gregg answered. "The recorders were hidden, and this is a high political figure."

Oscar sighed, "You might as well forget that, pal. He'd get you for entrapment, and you'd spend the rest of your life behind bars. If it's a congressman or a senator, you don't have a chance."

Gregg was disappointed, "Thanks. We'll go a different route. Keep in touch buddy."

They all looked at each other, and Mark asked, "Now what?"

"We can go after him, and he'll never know what hit him," Max offered.

Gregg shook his head, "No, there are too many on that Hill who will take his place. We're going to have to go bigger. I know many people agreed with the first round of demands from Peterson because of the bombings and the radiation. But we know that there was no radiation, and he is coming out with laws that make no sense and are hurting our citizens terribly. I'm willing to bet ninety percent or more of our citizens are not happy about him confiscating all the wealth our people had, and they would fight back themselves if they knew how to without being thrown in jail by this monster who is playing President. We have to come up with something big that is peaceful and will get rid of most of those in top government jobs. Think about it and what we can do. Let's meet back here tomorrow and see what kind of a plan we can come up with."

After his buddies left, a knock came on his front door. Gregg opened the door and saw an FBI agent. "Good afternoon, sir, I was sent to tell you that no remains of your wife were found at the explosion site. Either she was very near the explosive when it went off which would not allow any remains to be found or she wasn't in the building. As far as we know, she was on the list and was in the building with the others."

97

Gregg stood by the door and listened. He said nothing.

The agent continued, "I am very sorry to have to tell you that there are no remains of your wife. If you have any questions, please give me a call." The agent handed Gregg his business card and walked back to his car. Gregg left the card on the table by the door.

That evening, Gregg went to see Jody. She was watching the news and painting her toe nails when a knock came on the door.

"Hi Gregg," she smiled, "come on in."

"Got a visit from the FBI today," he smiled back at her. "They found no trace of Jamie, but he said if she had been close to the explosive when it went off there wouldn't be any traces of her."

"Where else could she have been if she wasn't in the building?" she started to think of other possibilities.

"He didn't say," Gregg told her. "He made it pretty plain that they believe she was in the building but was so close to the explosion they would find nothing. I don't know what to believe."

"Did they find everyone else?" Jody almost demanded an answer.

"That is a question I can ask him if I call him. He gave me his business card," Gregg looked at the TV.

"Well, I don't know how much longer I can work for that bastard," she turned the TV sound down. "He's driving me crazy, and he thinks the world revolves around him. You should see the way a lot of the other senators and congresspeople try to jockey for position. It's sickening. Not one word on Jamie, our people are treated like government issue, and they are only worried about their own asses."

"I'll bet you're tired of that," Gregg sympathized. "Please hang on though. I don't know for sure what we're going to do, but we have to come up with a plan to stop all of this. Our people are hungry and being forced to work for the rich. Our Constitution has been trashed by the political tyrants, and our rights are completely gone."

"How did it go with Seagly?" she asked.

"He couldn't help at all, and I'm not sure if it's because he doesn't have enough power to fight Peterson or if he plans on becoming one of them."

"Oh look," Jody picked up the remote to turn the sound back up, "the son-of-a-bitch is on TV again."

The East Room with a podium and microphone set up was flashed on the screen. A minute later, President Peterson was introduced.

"Good evening, everyone," Jacob began. "I would like to update you on the progress we have made on the necessary changes that were put into law.

It is my pleasure to let you know all of the permanent distribution centers have been set up and are working well. These sites will remain the purchasing points for all of your needs. The allotment cards have been distributed and are updated with credit according to the hours of work each person has accomplished. Most people are finding that their monthly credit amount exceeds the sum required to purchase all of their wants. Both of these accomplishments have been true successes.

Our production of food, non-food goods, and medicines is progressing nicely. We have run into a few kinks, but we are working tirelessly to fix the processes so they run smoothly. As we have discussed before, we are also supplementing our production by buying from other nations such as China. The foreign governments are working with us as true allies to make certain we obtain all we need.

The Distribution Agency is fully manned and can answer any questions or concerns you might have. Sixty-seven percent of able-bodied adults have been given their work assignments, and we expect one hundred percent assignment soon. For those who have not received their position within the next month, the military will be coming to see you to assist. By the end of the year, we expect to be on a seamless path to prosperity.

As you all know, we have been blessed with millions of immigrants to our great country. With the movement of our citizens from the radioactive areas and with the continuing inflow of people from around the world, we do not have enough housing for everyone in safe areas. I have just signed a new Executive Order making it law for our citizens to share their homes with those less fortunate. The National Guard and Army will be bringing persons to a suitable area and placing them in existing housing along with the owners of the homes. We must work together to ensure all people have a roof over their head, and to accomplish this we ask you to cooperate. Each household will receive from one to three new families to live with the owner. In this day and age, it is not important anymore to have a house or apartment for each family. The apartments all belong to the government now, so for those sharing your space with others, it will cost you nothing. Homeowners must realize this is the only way that we can accommodate all, so please welcome those who are brought to your door. The resources of all people in the household can be combined to create a comfortable environment. The language spoken by the family needing a home will determine what area they are brought to. This will continue until all housing is used effectively.

I would also like to point out that assisting all of our people will be a tremendous task, so the foreign military that is here to train will be helping in every area to ensure all are taken care of. Please be appreciative of their support.

Thank you for working hard to beat the terrorist attacks that tried to shut down our country and discourage our citizens. Our democracy demands that we all work together, and we appreciate each and every one of you."

Reporters started yelling questions, "How many families is each congressperson going to put in their home?" "What will you do with the people who refuse to take a job?" "How are we supposed to support every person in the world?" "How many families are the past presidents taking into their homes? They all have mansions that can hold many families."

After Jacob heard the types of questions being thrown out to him, he turned and left the podium without a word. Going back to his office, he met Lucy in the hallway. She gave him a summary of what was going on, "The phones have been ringing off the hook since you started your update. The Capitol switchboard is being bombarded as well. Everything you said has turned into a complaint from the people, and the biggest complaint is sharing their homes with strangers."

"Too damn bad," he responded. "As of tomorrow end of business, everyone who has not gotten a job assignment will be picked up and taken to one of the work camps. They had their chance, and if they don't want to work at what we were going to give them, then they can work putting in roads, sewers, or whatever else we need from the labor camps. The military can start packing homes with the homeless starting tomorrow morning. For years I've heard our citizens complain about many things, well they can stop complaining because this is the way it is going to be from this point forward. They weren't happy when they could run their own lives, so now they can exist with us running their lives for them."

Lucy was stunned at Jacob's attitude, "Maybe you should slow down just a bit."

"Alright," Jacob agreed. "Get ahold of our media outlets and tell them to let the people know that all we've talked about must be done to keep our democracy. If they are good citizens, they will follow directions and help our country get out of this. Tell them to shame their viewers into doing as they're told."

Lucy nodded and left his office. She was starting to wonder how their plans were finally going to fall apart. "This is going to get very messy soon," she thought.

Jody turned the TV off and shook her head, "What a slimy bastard. I'm telling you, Gregg, I can't stay there."

Gregg understood, "I know, but please trust us. We are somehow going to change this and put him where he belongs."

The next day, Gregg was sitting at his kitchen table going over a list he'd made out. "What if I don't think of everything? If we get caught setting this up, we'll be in prison for the rest of our lives with this government. Well if the guys don't want to go along, I understand, but I'm going to give it a try."

A quick knock came at his door, and his four buddies walked in and sat down at the table. Gregg gave them a quick nod.

"Did any of you come up with anything?" he asked them.

They all said no, so Gregg continued. "I've got a plan, but if you guys don't want to go along, I understand."

Leo smiled, "Let's hear it."

"I call it Operation Albatross."

"For the traitors in government and the burden they are putting on the people?" Max offered.

"Exactly," Gregg smiled. "We are going to honor the oath we took. Most veterans see that oath as binding even if they're out of the Service. This government has become rogue, and the top level throughout think they own our country and us."

Gunman looked at his buddies, "We're going to take on those bastards?"

"Not just us, but all patriotic vets and people of our great country. We have to do something, and after his speech last night I think most of our people will go with us."

"Okay," Max said, "how are we going to do that?"

Gregg smiled, "We're going to have to work through retired vets. That's the only way we'll have a chance to do anything. They are intertwined across the country and with the independent towns that are still not surrendering to the regime. So, they'll be the ones to help us. Most of them have a web of family, friends, and acquaintances who they can call on to spread the word. As we build on that, we'll see what other opportunities come up and we can expand from there."

"Are we going to attack?" Gunman was curious.

"Nope," Gregg said, "this is going to be completely peaceful, and we will get our government back."

"Okay," Gunman agreed, "tell us what to do."

Gregg went on, "We'll be contacting vets and people in the areas we came from. We'll make up a list of the people we know in our section of the country, so Leo, you take the southeast, and Max, you'll take the southwest.

Gunman, you'll be northwest, and Mark, northeast. I'll take the middle of the country. Be careful and feel out the people you call. If they are happy with what the government is doing, hang up because they aren't with us. There are always a few vets that do anything the government tells them to do. If they are sick of this government, then they'll be one of us. Those people will talk to others and so on. As the ball rolls along, more and more will talk to others who are against the politicians. I'm going to ask Oscar if he can help with a list of retired and short-term vets from all Services for the last ten or twenty years. That list will be divided up too, so each of us can use it. I have a couple of friends inside who I think will help us. They can send out messages to retired vets through their systems, and those messages won't be detected if they do it right. Those communications will have to interest those who want to take a stand so they read it, and those who aren't interested in changing things will disregard it. I'll have to figure out how we can do that with the guys who send the messages out. We'll have to be very careful. One or two whistleblowers and that will be it, so we have to be sensible and leave anyone out who is on the side of these bastards or who hates our country. If they sound like they hate what the government is doing, we enlist them to contact people in their area to work with us. This has to be nationwide. We do this for the next three months, and we tell them we'll all meet in D.C. on the first day of July. Make sure you have contact points to get ahold of in case something comes up. I'm hoping to get at least a million in D.C. July 1st."

Mark liked the idea, "We can make lists of the people we call, and those people can make lists of people they contact. This can work!"

"Yes," Gregg was sure it could work too, "but these are the rules we have to tell everyone we talk to. No one can bring a weapon, and we'll stay peaceful even if the government sends in their goons to cause trouble. When we get to D.C., we'll stop the city. No one will leave until we have resignations from all the officials who have to go."

"Alright," Max said. "Let's start making out lists of the people we'll talk to first. Use a computer to track who you've contacted. We'll add to the lists as we go along. The people we call will have to do the same. That way we can tell if we're anywhere near the number we want." They all nod in agreement.

Operation Albatross began that day.

CHAPTER TEN

Gunman got up early the next day and picked up his phone. "Hey Dave, it's Gunman. How's it going in Cheyenne? Things easy now you're out of the Service?"

"Hi buddy," his friend was glad to hear from one of his favorite pals he served with. "Hell no things aren't going good. The taxes they levy on our ranches are putting a lot of people out of business. Shit, in the last month I know of five ranchers who sold their acres, and they sold them to China. This keeps up, we won't have any land in this country that we own to grow food. What does that tell you. There's a place not far from here that has fences all around the land the Chinese bought and signs that say 'keep out'. Don't know for sure, but I've heard the Chinese are building a town in there and farming. I even heard they brought some of their slaves over to work the land."

"Anything but the taxes and Chinese?" Gunman wanted to make sure his friend was against the government.

"What in the hell is the government doing letting all of those drugs into the country? One of my friend's sons died from taking one pill, and there is a long list every week of people who have died from drug overdose just in our county," Dave was disgusted.

Gunman listened, and when his buddy had finished, he began, "Let me tell you why I called. We are going to start a march in D.C. to protest this government. We're going to work together to shut down the city until the officials that need to go resign."

"I would love to be part of that," Dave said.

"Good," Gunman continued. "We need you to spread the word to everybody you know who isn't a fan of the government. Make a list on your computer of everyone you contact, and ask them to make a list as well. By the last week of June, have them send you their lists. You can send me the number of those expected to protest, and we can combine from all of our contacts and see how many we think will join us. The march will begin the first day of July in D.C. And let everyone know that no weapons will be brought along. Peaceful march, and when the government troublemakers start, we'll quietly put them aside."

"Sounds good," Dave told his friend with hope in his voice, "I'll be in touch."

Max was a couple of miles away at his house calling Fred in San Antonio.

"Hello," Fred was on the line.

"Hey buddy, it's Max. How's San Antone?"

"Hi Max, good to hear from you! Not very good right now in all of Texas. We've got people from everywhere living in tents on the south side under bridges and along streets. Little kids running around half naked and hungry."

"Sounds like D.C.," Max told his friend.

"Lots of people have left their homes. It was too dangerous for them to stay where they were especially if it was a woman with children and no husband. Our citizens are treated like second class people down here too, and there isn't enough police enforcement to help. Some of the foreigners break into every house they come up to, and some attack the homeowners."

"I knew it was getting bad," Max said a little stunned, "but I didn't know it was that bad. I guess it's happening all over."

"Yeah," Fred agreed, "but most of them cross right here in Texas, and this has been going on for years now. Our politicians couldn't care less as long as they are safe and secure. Can't understand why neither side of government cares that our country is now sixty-five percent citizens or legal immigrants and thirty-five percent illegal immigrants from every culture and every language. And our citizens are paying to support most of the illegal immigrants and still many of our own. Our nation is floundering friend, and we won't be the same United States for long. We are quickly turning into a third world country."

"I agree, and that's why I called," Max began to tell Fred what the plan was and how important it was to stay away from those wanting our country to disappear. Fred understood and agreed to spread the word.

"I'll send you the numbers we have by the end of June," Fred told Max. "Thanks buddy, I have something to look forward to now. All of those I contact will be working hard for this. See you in D.C. on the first of July."

Gregg took a break from making calls and decided to see how Gunman was doing. "Hi Gunman, how's it going?"

"Shit it's crazy in Cheyenne," his friend began, "The taxes are killing the farmers, people are dying by the thousands from drug overdose, and the Chinese have bought up thousands of acres of land out there. My buddy told me the Chinese have put fences around all that land, and he thinks they've built a town and are farming. He believes they have slaves in there to do the work."

"Problems everywhere," Gregg sounded depressed.

"What are you finding out?" Gunman asked.

Gregg shook his head and answered his friend, "Lots of people losing family members with all of the crime and killings going on. Some of the cases are pretty sad. Tent cities with druggies all around. Poor kids living on the streets with nothing. Our government has set our people up really well. I guess they can stop yelling about discrimination because everyone of our people is in the same boat. And of course, the rich and politicians live awfully well in their secured mansions. Now the politician cares nothing about the people they promised equity to, and the focus is on making the rich richer and more powerful."

"Have you talked to Leo or Mark yet?" Gunman wondered.

"Not yet," Gregg answered. "I'm certain I'll hear nothing but problems in their areas too. Talk to you tomorrow."

Gregg started his normal pacing so he could think things through. He stopped long enough to leave a message for Oscar then started pacing again waiting for a return call. He decided to call his sister-in-law. "Hi Jody, it's me."

"Where have you been?" she asked.

"I've been busy working to start a march on D.C. to clean out this government."

Jody sounded alarmed, "You better be careful. Peterson is setting up lots of surveillance to catch anyone who disagrees with him. I just found out that he had the military set up rebel camps. I guess there are a number of them across the nation, and anyone who doesn't do things his way or causes any trouble goes to one of those guarded places."

Gregg remembered, "Yes, I've heard about those. Do you know where any of those camps are?"

"Not exactly," she said. "He keeps that information locked up. But I know that there are at least five around the country."

"Have you heard anything about the Chinese setting up cities out west?" he wondered.

She wasn't surprised, "No, but the politicians would treat that as top secret. They get too much money from foreign countries to let anything like that out and have our people demand the foreigners get off our land."

"Any chance you can get a list of the vets who have served in the last twenty years?" he was pretty sure she couldn't.

"No," Jody answered, "I don't know anyone who can do that. Look, when that march is going to start, let me know. I want to be involved."

Gregg chuckled, "Okay, will do."

Just as he put his phone down, a call came through. "Hi Gregg, it's Oscar."

Gregg smiled, "Hi Oscar. Got a question for you. Can you get me a list of all of the vets who served in the last twenty years?"

"Yeah, I think so," his friend was going through contacts in his head. "It's going to take me a few days though."

"Great," Gregg responded. "I've got a computer, so you can send me files with the names. I'll be watching for your email. Thanks buddy!"

Oscar hung up and flipped through his rolodex. "Nothing there," he said to himself. He pushed the button on his intercom to call his secretary. Once she answered, he told her to get Bruce Wilos on the line.

He leaned back in his chair wondering what his friend was going to do with a list of veterans. That type of list certainly wouldn't be classified, so Oscar saw no harm in giving out the information. "Maybe he's going to try and get vets together for some type of reunion," he thought. "Sure hope he's not looking for some type of trouble."

His secretary buzzed him back and told him Mr. Wilos was on line two. Oscar pushed the button, "Hey Bruce, how are you doing?"

"Great!" Bruce laughed. "When are you coming up to play golf? It's been over a year since I've seen that mug of yours."

Oscar laughed, "Too busy right now, bud. I do have a favor to ask though."

"Shoot," his friend encouraged him on.

"I need a list of the veterans for the last twenty years," Oscar knew he was asking for a big favor.

"Whoa," his friend was startled, "that's a big request."

"I know," Oscar chuckled, "but I'll owe you."

"Well that works out fine for me," Bruce agreed. "I know a guy who knows a guy. Give me a few days, and I'll have it delivered to your office."

"Thanks pal," Oscar smiled and hung up.

The next evening, Gregg was tired and threw his phone on the bed. "This is almost impossible," he thought. He laid down and stared at the ceiling wondering if it was even plausible to consider cleaning a despotic government out and replacing it with a fresh government that would be forced to follow the law or be held accountable. The people would have to stand behind this. But how many would not support the effort when they were being treated like serfs and every promise that had ever been made to them by the traitorous politicians had been broken. That included promises broken to every color, every culture, every profession, and every level of society except the very rich.

He sat up and called Mark. "Hi Mark, it's Gregg. How's it going?"

"Son-of-a-bitch, Gregg," his friend was shocked, "Remember the independent towns we talked about? I spoke to a man in Massachusetts who told me the citizens of their town had banded with those who moved in, and they were armed. Those who moved hid their weapons and then went back to get them. They have surrounded the city and refuse to let anyone in. The military is trying to get in to follow Peterson's directives, but the citizens keep telling them to go to hell."

"Yeah, I think more are doing that," Gregg said.

"That's what the guy said, and he told me they would get their guns out and fire on the military if they had to. They don't want anything to do with Peterson's new laws," Mark was excited.

Gregg exhaled, "That's good for us, but this is getting hotter quicker than I thought it would. Have you talked to many people yet?"

Mark looked at his list, "Yeah, lots of people, and they are all with us. How about you?"

"I've contacted lots of people in the towns I used to live in, and they are with us as well. I just don't know if that will be enough."

"There are lots of vets who are ready to take arms," Mark told his friend.

"That's no good," Gregg reminded Mark. "You've got to talk these people out of bearing any arms. They have to go peacefully or they'll spend the rest of their lives in prison."

Mark sighed slowly, "I'm trying. I keep telling them that, but you know vets. I think it'll be alright once we get together."

"Okay," Gregg sounded tired, "I'll be talking to you."

A few days later, Oscar was in his office after hours, and a knock came on the outside office door. He walked through his secretary's office and opened it. A delivery man handed him a yellow envelope and started to walk away, so Oscar thanked the man quickly and went back to his office. He opened the envelope and found a letter from Bruce. "Here you go. Remember you owe me!" Oscar laughed and took the thumb drive out of the little container and slid it into his computer.

"Good deal," Oscar thought. "Let's see, Gregg gave me his email address before. Here it is." He copied the files to an email and sent it off to his friend. "Hope this is what you need, Gregg. I better text him and let him know he's got the files."

Gregg heard a message come in, so he picked up his phone. "Good job Oscar! Thanks buddy!" he wrote back to the friend he owed a very large debt to.

107

He started his computer and saw just what he wanted to see, thousands of names. Gregg knew many of the people had probably died, but there would be many who would be around to help their cause.

Smiling, he called Leo.

"What's up?" Leo answered the phone.

"We're doing a good job," Gregg answered, "but we can't get word out fast enough. Oscar got a long list of vets, so we'll call a few in each big city and send the lists from that area to them so they can call too. We can each talk to a few of these people so we can be sure they're safe."

"Okay," Leo agreed, "I'll call some."

Gregg smiled as his robust friend got excited, "Good. You call Mark and Max, and I'll get Gunman. We'll make my house the headquarters and start tomorrow morning."

"Will do!" Leo said with enthusiasm.

That answer gave Gregg a feeling of victory. If they could muster that type of passion from the people, there would be a clear path to win the battle for their freedom. Gregg watched people every day as he went about his business, and the faces of the people told the story. Hardly a smile was seen anymore, and kids were no longer children, but they had to become adults quickly in order to survive. The idea of having morals was unimportant to the ones pushing chaos and evil. The people were tired of needless killing, constant crime, destroyed lives because citizens disagreed with the establishment, and the endless preying on illegals who were unskilled and uneducated. The masses still wanted a country driven by principles and justice. Unfortunately, unscrupulous media got away with making people feel helpless and hopeless. If citizens didn't go along with the evil agenda, they were made to feel ashamed of themselves and pointed out as unfit for society.

Gregg knew the nation would become a third world country in a short amount of time unless something was done. He wondered how people so insistent on pushing the ideals of the government's top layer would look at life once they became part of the serf system and had no say at all. Those at the top of the regime and the rich didn't care anything about anyone but themselves, and those who supported them would one day be awfully disappointed when they were betrayed by those they saw as heroes.

He turned on his TV and saw that Peterson was once again going to address the nation. "I wonder what bullshit he is going to try and pull this time," Gregg thought.

Peterson stood at the podium in the East Room with his normal sidekicks around him. Those who followed everything Jacob said and would lick his boots to get ahead.

Jacob began, "Good evening, everyone. I would like to start off by thanking everyone for all of the support we have received making all that has been accomplished possible. I know that all of our citizens realize these changes are needed to ensure our country continues to function unhampered. We received a great deal of input concerning the distribution centers and jobs that have been given out. Most are very pleased with the results.

Also, we have determined from the great need across our country that more military will be needed to maintain law and order. To this end, when each of our children reaches the age of eighteen, they will automatically be enlisted in the military where they will be educated further and trained. Our kids will work beside the foreign military that is here, and in that way, they can learn from each other. Our citizens will serve for four years, and then they will each be given a lifetime job to support themselves. This will allow us to have peace continuously.

Because of the excellent support we have received from foreign nations such as China, we have invited several of our foreign supporters to move some of their businesses to our country. They will be able to assist in drilling oil and gas, increasing our agricultural outputs, producing needed batteries and chips, and contributing much more by buying and using our assets effectively with their years of professional training. With their businesses owning and running many of these functions in our country, we will not have to worry about shortages any longer. We hope that all of our citizens appreciate the great work their government has accomplished for us.

To ensure you all know what is going on daily in our country, this Administration is going to immediately take over and run all media avenues including television and internet. By doing this, everyone will have the capability to find out what is really going on daily by written or spoken word in their own language. As you can see, we are a team and can do anything. We have beaten the terrorists who tried to defeat our country and our people! Thank you."

A newscaster came on immediately after Peterson left the podium, "We are very lucky to have great leadership," he said. "Our President is ensuring that we keep our great country, and he is placing the correct guiding posts for our people so everyone knows what to do, when to do it, and how to do it. He certainly is the master planner for our nation."

Gregg turned the TV off and wondered how Peterson could even address the people after what he had done. He had actually turned the country into a communist nation and sold every citizen out to foreign nations.

The next morning, Gregg laid in bed a little while before getting up and making coffee. Going to the front porch, he picked up the paper and looking through it quickly folded it up and pitched it into the garbage. True to his word, the articles were written by Jacob's flunkies who communicated to the public what they wanted them to think. Gregg expected them to repeat their messages over and over until they became part of citizens' thinking patterns. A deadly performance by the government to condition people to do what they were told at the command of the regime.

Gregg called Jody, "Did you see what our leader said yesterday? Is he kidding?"

"Hi Gregg," Jody sounded depressed. "No, unfortunately he's not kidding. He is making certain we understand he is in control."

"We're going to need your help, Jody," Gregg knew what he was asking could hurt her.

"I'll be glad to help anyway I can," she said as if she was determined to get back at Peterson.

"Do you have any friends you can trust who can help us after work?"

Jody snickered, "I quit. I just couldn't stand it anymore, and every time Peterson walked by me my skin crawled. Most of the friends I had at the White House and at the Capitol quit too because of that bastard."

"Okay," Gregg was kind of surprised. "Can you come to my house? Bring them with you. We have lots of work to do!"

That same morning, Leo got up and went out to get his mail. He started going through the envelopes as he walked back into his house, and suddenly he stopped. There was a letter from the government, so he opened it up and read it. He called Gregg.

"Hey Gregg, it's Leo."

"Hi, when will you be over?"

Leo started to laugh, "Listen to this. I got a letter from the government telling me to report to work at a production facility a few blocks from here. They can kiss my ass."

"Come on over pal," Gregg smiled. "I imagine we'll all get one of those. I'll make you breakfast, and we can wait for the others to get here."

By late morning, all of the guys had gotten to Gregg's, and Jody and her friends were there too. His living room was full, so he stood in the middle and thanked them all for coming. "Glad you're all here. Thanks, Jody, for bringing some help because we have got lots of work to do."

Gunman added, "Those bastards are killing our people. Peterson said people were getting enough credit to feed themselves. He's crazy. They are going hungry everywhere except the places that are fending for themselves and telling him to go to hell. I imagine they will disappear soon and be put into some of those rebel camps. This is getting really bad fast."

"I'm surprised the people just take it and do what they're told," Max shook his head. "Taking kids away from their families and giving people jobs to support the rich and politicians while they go hungry. What has to happen to get these people to take a stand and make Peterson and those with him accountable for what they're doing?"

"We all feel the same way," Gregg agreed, "but we have to stay low key right now. We don't want any of them to get wind of this until it's too late to stop us. Now, Oscar sent me a list of all of the vets for the last twenty years. I sorted them by city, and then I printed off these pages. We all have to pick names from the lists and call them. Tell them you're a vet and ask them how things are going in their town. If they act like the government is doing a good job, hang up. If they start swearing and want to get rid of these bastards, they are the ones we want. Tell them what we're doing and we'll start the march the first day of July in D.C. Send them the list for their city. Ask them to track who they contact."

Leo was ready to go, "We are going to get a lot of help that way. They'll tell their families, and the word will spread from there. Lots of patriotic people in this country."

Gregg continued, "I contacted several guys I know at the Veteran's Affairs Office. They are going to mass email retired vets under the radar and let them know by a type of code they'll understand that we are forming groups to come to D.C. on the first day of July for a protest. No weapons, but we will peacefully take back our nation."

"What happens when the government finds out, which they will," Gunman looked at his friends.

They all knew Gunman was right, so Gregg said, "We'll see who they target. If we have a choice, I'll take the rap. Whatever happens, the rest of us must continue calling. Do you all understand?"

Jody smiled, "Yeah, we understand, and we can't wait to get that son-of-a-bitch and put him before a jury of citizens he has hurt and ruined to be held accountable. What are we going to do once the march starts?"

Gregg looked thoughtfully into space and without hesitation said, "We're going to take our country back."

CHAPTER ELEVEN

Months went by, and all of them worked hard every day. Gregg's house looked like a war zone, and some of them started to get discouraged, others appeared angry, and some were just tired.

"I think it's going good, guys," Gregg told them all. "We know all the independent cities are with us too. Peterson is stepping up his takeover tactics on them."

Gunman agreed, "I got through to a lot of people. Almost all of them are pissed off at what's going on, and they just don't know what to do about it. I think they'll join us."

"I'm getting the same thing," Leo looked at all of the paper around him. "I hope they're all serious and really mean what they say. If they all contact the people on the lists we sent and they and their families and friends come, we're going to swamp that city."

Mark looked up as if he almost forgot, "Hey, I talked to a guy who asked me how we're going to let the world know what's going on once people get to D.C. His name is Pete, and he was an anchorman on one of the news channels. He quit because he wasn't going to spread Peterson's propaganda, but he said he knows people who will support us. He can get his friends to film the march and what's being said and broadcast it for the world to see. By the time the regime's goons get there, it will be too late to stop the dissemination. That's a great opportunity to expand this thing nationwide while we're protesting."

"He's a brave man," Gregg was pleased. "That is fantastic! I was trying to figure out how we could do that. Do you think he's legit? Does he realize that if he does do that and our plan doesn't work, he'll be put in the deepest, darkest dungeon they have?"

Mark grinned, "I already asked around about him, and his story checked out. Hopefully he will do what he says he'll do."

"We're taking a lot of chances," Gunman was concerned. "We are trusting too many people, and something is bound to go wrong." After a minute he added, "Guess we'll trust the Man upstairs to lead the charge. He's done it before, and I never doubt Him."

"You know, Gregg," Leo looked at his friend, "you'll be the speaker in D.C., so maybe we should all have a copy of the speech you're going to give just in case."

"You're right, Leo," Gregg looked at his longtime friend with a brotherly love that is hard to find. "I better get that written out. No matter what happens, the rest go on with the march. We'll pick up the pieces later."

"Once we get the march together, we're going to have to have shifts of people to watch for the government thugs who'll make trouble," Max knew how their troublemakers worked. "They have to be taken care of right away so the march doesn't turn into a free-for-all."

The women sat there listening to all that the men said. Looking at each other, Jody asked the question all the women were wondering, "If we get caught and taken to a camp, the ones who are free will come and get us won't they?"

Leo looked at them and understood instantly. He and the guys were used to planning operations, and they knew what consequences could come. These women had never served in any of the Services, and of course they wouldn't know what to do if the protest didn't turn out like they thought it would. He smiled at them, "Hopefully that won't be a problem, but yeah, we'll come and get you. Don't worry, Jody, but stay away from us during the march. We'll be the targets."

"I can't promise I'll stay away from the main action," Jody told them. "We still don't know about Jamie for sure, and I want to see Peterson go down."

The next day before Leo left to go to Gregg's, an unmarked FBI car with two plainclothes men parked just down the street from his house. Dan, the agent with more experience, told his partner, "Let's just knock on the door and ask to talk to him. If he's an asshole, we shove our way in."

His partner, Cliff, agreed, "Just remember we can't go back empty handed. They are madder than hell and want people like this put out of business." He looked at Dan and meant it. Cliff was fully behind Peterson and loved to bully any citizen he could. Dan liked to go by the book, so he definitely didn't want to break the law.

The FBI agents stepped up onto Leo's porch and knocked on the door. Leo was just finishing getting dressed when he heard the rap at the front of the house. "Who in the hell is it?" He opened the door, "Yeah, what do you want?"

"Just want to talk to you, sir," Cliff answered.

"Who are you?" Leo asked suspiciously.

Cliff flashed his badge, and Leo was on alert immediately. He opened the door and let the two enter.

"We would like to ask you some questions about why you're contacting retired vets," Dan told him.

"I called a couple of buddies I served with, why?" Leo looked at them skeptically.

Cliff moved closer to Leo, "These weren't your buddies. In fact, they didn't even know you."

"Well maybe I dialed the wrong number," Leo stood confidently, "or maybe I was trying to make new friends."

Dan started to lose his patience, "Look it shit head we know you're trying to get people together to complain about the new government. You've called lots of people, and a couple of them told us you were trying to find out how they felt about this Administration."

"New government?" Leo acted surprised. "This isn't just a temporary thing until the radiation scare is over? This Administration formed a new government?"

Cliff got in Leo's face, "Why are you calling vets?"

"I told you," Leo smiled, "I'm looking up old buddies."

"You're going to have to come with us," Dan told him. "We need to take you downtown for questioning."

"Is it against the law to talk on the phone?" Leo smiled.

They escorted Leo out to their car and put him in the back. No one spoke as they drove down to FBI Headquarters. Once they got into the building, they went to Cliff's office. They told Leo to sit down at a table and then showed him a transcript. Someone had called in and told them that a march was being planned and calls were being made to get people to join.

"Who made the call?" Leo asked after reading the document. "I don't know anything about a march. I told you I called a buddy."

Dan pushed the transcript away, "Well this buddy thinks you're looking for trouble."

Leo sat at the table and ignored the two agents. Cliff got fed up and slugged Leo in the face.

"You son-of-a-bitch," Leo said dabbing at the blood running down from the side of his mouth.

"Shut up you little bastard," Cliff snapped. "Do you really think you're going to go up against the new government? Do you?" he started laughing.

Dan tried to calm things down, "Look it Leo, we know what you've been calling people about. Who else is involved with this?"

Leo turned his head away from his persecutors, "I don't know what you're talking about."

Dan and Cliff fired off more questions, but Leo was tired of answering, so he sat there and looked at them. Finally, Cliff started to threaten him.

"We're going to have to take you to a labor camp until you decide you want to talk to us," Cliff taunted Leo.

Leo gave him a dirty look, "I have rights, and I haven't done anything wrong. You can't hold me."

"Watch us," and then Cliff started to hit and kick their target. Leo was fed up with the treatment, so he fought back and got Cliff on the floor. Dan tried to break it up, and when he got Leo to his feet, Cliff pulled his revolver and shot him. Leo hit the floor dead.

"What in the hell did you do that for?" Dan was outraged. "He was just protecting himself!"

"Screw that, he was trying to escape. These punks have to be put down now," Cliff was almost out of control. "You know there are lots more of these idiots out there, and if we have to, we'll take them down one by one just like we did this stupid bastard."

Dan just shook his head and called for an ambulance. "How in the hell are we going to explain this? Shit, the way things are going maybe it really doesn't matter what we do or say."

Dan and Cliff went their separate ways for the rest of the morning. They both knew that they had to go out again and find more of the people accused of forming a march to protest the government, so they had to calm down and cool off. After lunch, they met up again and went out to their car to begin the afternoon hunt.

The others hadn't come back from lunch yet, so Gregg was home alone calling people on the list he had. He saw a car pull up slowly in front of his house from the kitchen window. Not recognizing it, he became suspicious immediately. After a few minutes, a knock came on the door, so Gregg went to the front door and opened it. The two men started to step inside before they were invited in, so Gregg stood in front of the door and asked, "Who are you guys?"

Cliff and Dan showed Gregg their badges and asked to come in. Gregg moved to the side. Dan pulled out a picture and showed it to Gregg, "Do you know this man?"

"Yeah," Gregg shrugged, "he's a buddy of mine."

"Do you know anything about a protest march that is being planned?" Cliff asked. They stood quietly staring at Gregg waiting for an answer.

Gregg returned the stare calmly, "Don't know anything about that."

"Have you talked to this buddy recently?" Dan flipped the picture of Leo back into view.

"A few days ago," Gregg stared back at them.

Cliff looked at him as if he was a liar, "But you don't know anything about what he's been doing?"

"No," Gregg was firm and calm.

The two agents started moving around the room, "Mind if we look around?"

Cliff started to walk towards the kitchen, and Gregg stepped in front of him. "Yeah, I do mind. You got a search warrant?"

Cliff stood nose to nose with Gregg. After a few seconds, Cliff pushed Gregg, but Dan stepped in immediately. "No, we don't have a warrant. Thank you for your time. We may be back to talk to you again." He grabbed Cliff's arm and pushed him towards the door. They left the premises and got back into their car.

Dan looked at Cliff with disgust, "You ignorant asshole. We are not going to get anywhere with you acting like that. Call in and have them put a guy outside his house."

Gregg calmed himself down because he knew he had to start thinking strategically. "How did the FBI find out about Leo, and where was he? He should have been here this morning. How much does the FBI know? They knew about me too or they wouldn't have paid me a visit." The girls weren't coming back, so he decided to call Jody and make certain she was alright. He called her number, but it went to her voicemail.

Right then, the guys walked in. They looked at Gregg as if he was sick or something. "I just had a visit from the FBI. They've got Leo, and they came here to see what I know. They wanted to search the house, and I've got the lists on the kitchen table."

Gunman sat down, "Where have they got Leo? When are they going to let him go?"

"I don't know. Listen, in four days the march starts at the Capitol. We are going to have to disappear from here and not use our cell phones again. Sure as shit they're listening, and I don't know if they know about you guys or not."

Max looked out the window, "You do know there's a surveillance car outside your house."

Gregg looked out the window. "They're getting info on you guys right now," Gregg was thinking as he talked. "You came in the front, so they saw you. I know they didn't leave any bugs in here; they never got out of my sight. It is possible they've already taken pictures of all of you and are putting those in their system. The only way we can get away from them is to wait until it's dark and leave one by one. Gunman, your car isn't here, so we'll go to your house."

"I almost forgot," Mark added, "Pete, the anchorman I told you about, called me just a few minutes ago. He wants to meet all of us at his house tonight. Says he has something to show."

"Okay," Gregg agreed, "after we get to Gunman's car, we'll go see him. We'll have to stop at Roman's restaurant so I can call Jody and make sure she's alright. When we're done at Pete's, we are going to have to split up and use pay phones to call our contact points in each state. We need to know what to expect when we get into D.C. One call per pay phone and then we move along. We don't know if the FBI knows the day we start the march or not, and we can't have the people planning to come into D.C. frightened off."

Each of the guys had their lists and their contact points, so Gregg went into the kitchen and got all of his stuff together. Patiently they waited for the cover of darkness to come.

The stars were shining brightly when Gunman slid out the back door. There were a few street lights, but he was able to stay in the shadows making him almost impossible to see. After a few minutes, Max did the same. Finally, they were all out of Gregg's house and walking through backyards stealthily as if they were ghosts.

When they were four blocks away from Gregg's place, they came together and walked the two miles to Gunman's house. Hidden in the shadows, they looked for an FBI surveillance car. They split up and walked around the adjoining blocks to make sure no one was watching them. Once they knew everything was fine, they met up on Gunman's back porch.

"We're clear," Gunman said. "I've got the keys, so let's go."

They stopped at Roman's, and Gregg went inside to call his sister-in-law. "Hi Jody, I got your voicemail when I called before. Everything alright?"

"Yes, I'm fine. The others went home, but we plan to meet again at your house tomorrow morning," she told him.

"You can't do that. There's a FBI car setting outside my house, and they've got Leo. We don't know when they're going to release him. I wanted to let you know not to go to my house and don't call my cell phone. They're listening and tracking I'm certain, so the guys and I are going to call our contacts from pay phones. Sure hope we have a large enough group planning on being here in a few days. Tell your friends they are done for now and stay home. I don't want you arrested, so watch it on TV."

"You aren't going home anymore before then?" she was starting to get worried.

"We'll be fine, Jody. We just have to stay out of sight so the fed can't pick us up. I plan on being in front of the Capitol at noon." Gregg hung up and felt like he just lost an important person in his life. "I'll see her again. I know I will."

Gregg got back in the car, and Mark gave Gunman the address. They were all stunned when they drove into the Georgetown neighborhood. "Are you sure you got the right address?" Gunman asked Mark.

"Yeah, this is the address Pete gave me," Mark looked around surprised like the rest of them.

They pulled up in front of a beautiful mansion, and the four guys wondered what they were getting themselves into. They looked around expecting security to appear and ask them what they were doing there, but when no one came, they got out of the car and went up to the door.

Pete opened the door immediately and asked the group to come in. He was smiling as he introduced everyone to Richard, an ex-FBI agent. Mark introduced his friends, and they all went into the living room.

"Nice place," Max said feeling a little suspicious about where they were. "Is someone in your family in politics?"

"No" Pete said. "You don't have to worry; I'm not setting you up. My father was a university professor. One of the few who was very respected and taught the truth instead of a story someone else told him to tell. I followed in his footsteps when it came to telling the truth, only I followed a news career after my service to our country ended. I really admire what you guys are doing. I know that the government has taken over all of the media, but I have some friends who were shut down from broadcasting but still have the capability. They are willing to broadcast what you do in D.C around the world for as long as they can get away with it. I think Mark said you are all meeting up on the first of July. So, what is the daily itinerary for this event, and how long do you think it will last? They will want to start broadcasting when it is beneficial for people to see exactly what is happening. The first day or so may not be newsworthy with people still coming into town."

Gregg answered for his group, "We really don't have a daily itinerary. The first day we expect people to start congregating in D.C. They will be coming from all over the country, and so we believe that each day the crowd will increase. Once there are enough people in D.C. to stop everything, we are going to demand resignations."

Richard looked at Pete then at the others. "I quit the FBI because of this crooked Administration. I know how nasty these people are, and I can tell you that they won't think twice about killing anyone. They will do anything necessary to reach their goal of complete power. But the FBI isn't the only agency working towards this. The CIA, DOJ, and many others also want power over the people."

Richard stopped for a few seconds then continued. "As you probably know, the judicial system in many instances has been working for the party of their choice instead of going by the law. And the military is at their disposal as well, so you can see the people are confused and don't know what to do to change this around."

"They've got one of our buddies right now," Gunman said, "and we don't know when we'll see him again. They came after us too, but we aren't going to backdown. We were all special ops in the Marines, and we aren't scared, so we'll be seeing this thing through."

Pete smiled again, "I was special ops too. Sorry we never met or got to work together. With what we found out we're going to need special ops skills. I've been following guys who are involved with the rebel camps. They don't know I'm watching, and I can tell you that it's nasty. Richard told me about a couple other camps that they call labor camps. I don't know what the difference is between the two, but they're more like concentration camps, and I'm sure they murder a lot of people there. Richard has contacts who are still working inside the FBI but hate the regime just like we do. He can help us with intelligence and perhaps with getting more people into D.C. for the protest."

"Anything I can do I certainly will," Richard nodded at the group. "This government has to be stopped now. If we don't succeed, our country is gone for good."

Pete turned to the TV. "This is what I filmed today before I called you, Mark." He started a video, and they all watched as they saw military guarding people inside a camp encircled by razor wire. "As I filmed, I noticed that the military at these camps consist of ours and foreign troops. It's like they are combining the forces with no distinction."

The prisoners who came on the screen were outside cutting wood, tending to small gardens, and doing various types of work. In the background, they could see large buildings set off in the distance. "What are those buildings?" Max asked.

Richard responded, "Those buildings are used for manufacturing different things. Some are for ammunition for the military, some are manufacturing cloth to be made into clothing, and believe it or not, in one of those buildings the organs of live people are harvested."

Everyone turned to look at Richard. "Yes," he said, "you heard me right. If anyone has a defect or is very sick but the organs are in good shape, the organs are removed and put on ice for shipping. Our government makes quite a bit off of this. It doesn't matter if they are citizens, illegals, children, or young adult, and if they have more requests than availability of the sick or disabled, people go missing so the quota can be met. Once they are finished with a body it goes into a pile, and at the end of each day the corpses are dumped in a ravine and covered. This goes on continuously."

"The people in these camps are those who spoke out against the government?" Max asked.

"Those and others who the government has no need for anymore. I know for a fact some politicians who are forced out end up there so they can't talk. A variety of people like newscasters who don't agree with the regime, a few of the rich who changed sides, and lots of homeless who were mainly from the rich peoples' suburbs end up at one of these camps."

"We knew a reporter who got an interview with Phineous Handler. The ex-Congressman communicated a lot about this government," Gregg told his new friends.

Pete looked at him, "I'll bet he's not around anymore."

Gregg nodded, "Handler died and the reporter was murdered."

"Don't be so sure Handler wasn't murdered too," Richard said matter-of-factly. "The regime has people of all classes and professions who work for them. If Handler's doctor found out he was talking, he just might have decided the retired Congressman needed some special medication."

"But that's not all they do in those buildings at all of the camps," Richard went on. "The food that is given out at the distribution centers comes from these places. If you ever look at the packaging, you would see that there are no ingredients listed. Nutrients are shown, but that is all. You see, the regime knew it would be cheaper to feed the people by using a little grain and mixing various things such as slugs, worms, maggots, insects, or anything that they could mass produce or obtain in high quantity into the food to keep those alive who could work and make products for the regime to sell and make money. Of course, the rich and the Administration have blue ribbon beef, pork, chicken, and other delicacies grown for their use as well as delicious fruits and vegetables. Nothing is too good for the evildoers of our world today who kill without remorse, abuse without a thought, and immorally think of no one but themselves and their desires."

"Our people are being fed filth? How come those processing that don't get the word out?" Max was outraged.

"Because they know they would be killed," Richard looked him in the eye, and everyone felt the chill of hopelessness those in the camps must be experiencing.

The group started watching the video again, and they saw people walking back and forth and the military pushing, hitting, and dragging people around who they thought didn't move fast enough. All of a sudden, Gregg stood up, "Stop the video. Rewind it!"

The rest of them looked at him as if he was crazy. Pete rewound the tape a little bit and started playing it again.

"Right there!" Gregg yelled.

Pete stopped the tape so they could all see what he saw. "That's Jamie, my wife!" Gregg exclaimed. "She's not dead. She looks tired and sad, but she's not dead! Come on, we're going to get her. Where's this camp?"

"Wait a minute guy," Pete put his hand up. "Those soldiers are trained to shoot anyone who tries to get in there. Watch this."

Pete fast forwarded to another part of the film. "I was lucky to catch this from behind a big tree late this afternoon. I was scared to death someone would see me, but I knew it was a big chance to show people what is going on."

As the film proceeded, they saw a truck back up to a ditch and dump its load into the trench. "Shit, those are the bodies you were talking about." Max looked sick to his stomach.

They continued watching as fifty or so bodies bounced into the gully. A couple of the corpses landed on the top rim, and Gregg and his buddies gasped as they saw Leo lying there dead.

"Those murdering bastards. Where did you tape this?" Mark demanded to know.

"Up in Maryland," Pete answered. "Look, I've only just started to find out all they are doing to our people."

"We have to get Jamie out of there before she ends up like Leo," Gregg was distraught after seeing just a glimpse of what was going on.

"The military is so thick around there you don't have a chance," Pete told him.

"Look Gregg," Gunman put a hand on his friend's shoulder, "you have to stay in D.C. and lead this march. No one else can do that. We've been friends for a long time and served together, so trust me to get her. Once we have her, we'll join you at the march." Gunman gave his buddy a steady stare, and Gregg knew he was right. "It's going to take us a couple of days to go there and plan a route in and out. We have to watch the guards and know their routine. By the time we get her, you'll be leading people to stop this madness."

Gregg knew Gunman could get Jamie. When they served together, Gunman was the one who could read a situation better than anyone else and figure out how to fix it or destroy it. He gave Gunman a faint smile and took his car keys. Mark, Max, and Gregg left Pete's house to get ready for the march that was to start soon.

Gunman turned to Pete. "Hope you're willing to help me. It'll be dangerous, but we can pull this off." Pete gave his new friend a smile.

CHAPTER TWELVE

The Chairman of the Joint Chiefs stood in Jacob's office and waited for him. Dick knew this would not be a fun meeting, but it was a meeting that had to be done. Peterson was surprised when he walked in and saw his friend waiting.

"Hi Dick, what's up?" Jacob smiled.

"Sir, we have an intelligence report that a mass of people will congregate in D.C. in two days to protest this government. This will be a march by people from across the nation, and I'm afraid it is going to be a protest with the goal of disbanding this Administration."

"You just found this out today?" Jacob couldn't believe that.

"We had indications before. Now we know that the FBI was aware of the situation, but they thought they could stop it before it started. Apparently, this march is being run by veterans, and many of the marchers will be veterans and their families."

Jacob sat down and tried to figure out what to do next. He called his Chief of Staff in and told him what was going on.

The Chief of Staff told them what to do immediately. "We'll send out word on all of the media avenues that anyone attending any protest march will be immediately arrested and tried for insurrection. We will stress that any rebellion will be looked at as treason and harsh punishment will be the judicial solution for this type of offence."

Jacob liked his solution and told him to begin the messages immediately. Then he turned to Dick. "Do you have any idea who the leaders are? If we can get rid of them, that and the messages through the media will stop this ridiculous revolt by the people. We'll be able to settle them down and get them back on the track of serving us."

"Once the FBI started looking into this, the organizers of the march found out and stopped using personal devices and started using a private code through public means. We have multiple names, but we don't have the evidence to arrest them," Dick waited for further instructions.

"Evidence?" Jacob scowled at his friend. "We don't need any evidence to arrest anyone. If they look suspicious to us, we will imprison them and they will stay there as long as we please. Give those names to the FBI and tell them to arrest all on the list immediately." Dick gave the President a salute and left his office.

Jacob wasn't satisfied with trusting the FBI to get this done. He looked out of the window and saw the Washington Memorial. "I know, I'll use the military." He picked up his phone and called the guard shack. "Intercept the Chairman of the Joint Chiefs and send him back."

Dick saluted again when he reentered Jacob's office. The President told him to sit down. "I want special ops working to find these bastards. I also want the Capitol and White House surrounded by military carrying guns. That should scare off a lot of them. We need helicopters watching from above, and troops must be stationed all around town. We'll have to send our people in to start fights, and then the military and FBI can take the marchers to jail. Make certain all of our people know who is on our side in the crowd so they aren't arrested and can keep working. Also, I don't want any of the march shown on TV or reported on the radio or the internet. The quieter we keep it, the less damage will be done. Do you think you can manage all of this?"

"Yes sir," Dick told him. He waited to see if Jacob had any other requests, but Jacob got interested in some paperwork on his desk. Dick got up, saluted, and left.

Two days later Gregg, Max, and Mark were at the Capitol mingling with others there to protest. Several thousand people had shown up already. "This is a start," Gregg said. "We'll see how this group grows over the next couple of days. I wonder if Peterson's threats across the media will stop people from coming."

The patriots who gathered wore smiles and held small United States flags. All of them were excited and ready to march anywhere they were needed, and none showed any signs of being intimidated by Peterson's Administration. Gregg noticed that more and more people were joining those already there. People were beginning to set up tents on the National Mall, and lots of protestors brought food that they were more than willing to share. It was apparent those who came were setting up to stay as long as necessary to change the government back to an asset for the people and one that would follow the Constitution. As more and more people poured in, the police and military in the area knew it was useless to try and arrest so many. The Mayor of D.C. watched from her office and ordered hundreds of portable toilets placed around the city so the Capital of the United States didn't turn into a huge bathroom.

Gregg looked at his buddies, "You two are going to have to watch for troublemakers. I don't know when it's going to start, but the government goons will show up. Any trouble spots won't be coming from our people, so we're going to have to enlist more men to work with us. When the trouble begins, the ones starting it have to be taken down and out of the crowd."

"I know there are some good vets here," Max told them. "I'll see if some of them will join in, and then we can spread the word so we have people all over watching for problems. These guys will know how to stop them."

People continued to join the march. Subways were packed, and they got off at the Capitol South and Smithsonian Metro stations adding more and more energy to the protest. Trains and buses were full. Cars were left in adjoining states, and people rode in together or waited for empty trains and buses to return for them.

Gregg and Mark talked to people as they walked along. They stayed by the Capitol and waited for Max to come back. A man on a bicycle pulled up alongside them and smiled, and they saw Max trotting behind him. "Hi," the man said lifting up a large cloth bag. "My buddy, Nick, brought these along. He thought they could help us keep in contact all over the city. There are twenty more bags like this."

Gregg looked inside and took out a walkie talkie. Max caught up to the man and laughed, "These guys know what they're doing. There are twenty of these things in each bag. We have some people on bikes and some on segways, and they are scoping out the leaders and the groups who came from the same state. These are being handed out so we can communicate from one end of the city to the other. We can direct people and really have a coordinated protest. The guys with the bags are also spreading the word about taking care of troublemakers. I think we have that pretty well under control with all the help we're getting. This march is awesome, and everybody keeps telling me there are lots more people coming. We are going to do it!"

More and more tents were going up, and people from D.C. were inviting those coming in for the march to stay at their houses. Everyone seemed to sense that they were part of something big, and they were right.

Gregg told Mark and Max to go get some sleep in the hotel room they had rented, and he would leave later to get some rest. "The next couple of days will tell us if we have enough people to let this regime know we aren't kidding."

His friends agreed and told him he needed sleep too. Gregg stayed for a while longer and then went to the hotel. He couldn't stop wondering where Pete and Gunman were and if they had a plan to get Jamie yet.

At that moment, Gunman and Pete were hiding behind a dumpster. They had waited for nightfall and then slowly worked their way up near a fence. Nothing was said, but Gunman handed Pete a pair of night vision goggles. They watched the movement of the camp and the time of the change of guard. Slowly they moved around the perimeter of the camp to see where most of the in and out traffic came from. They found two gates that looked like they were used very little, and they were on opposite sides of the camp. They saw very few guards around, but the ones they saw all had guard dogs with them which complicated things. When the inmates were all locked in the barracks, the soldiers put the dogs away and met by the main gate to tell jokes and laugh. Gunman and Pete left to go to their hotel planning to get back the next morning to watch the daily routine.

While Gunman cleaned his gun, he told Pete, "We have to find out what barrack Jamie is in tomorrow, so we'll watch during the day until we find her and follow her until she goes in for the night." Pete agreed, and they both finished getting ready for the next day.

The next morning, they were at the camp before sunrise. Positioning themselves in some thick brush that was higher than most of the camp, they could see the movement outside of the buildings. Both men were familiar with this kind of surveillance, and they made themselves comfortable.

The people started coming out of the barracks and went into a larger building where they would eat breakfast before starting their day. "Glad I don't have to eat the shit they serve in there," Gunman thought as he remembered what Richard had said.

As the people started leaving the mess hall, Gunman spotted Jamie and pointed her out to Pete. She would be the target of their surveillance until they got her. Jamie and twenty others followed a guard to a large vegetable garden, and the group started their daily work. The two observed other groups of prisoners around the camp doing other tasks, and as the day went on the temperature increased making the air sweltering. The soldiers guarding the groups yelled for the workers to go faster. One man asked for a drink, and the guard hit him in the face with the butt of his gun. Finally, it was time for them to stop for lunch.

"It's pretty brutal out here to work in the hot sun all day," Pete said as he watched the people file into the mess hall.

Gunman sighed, "The guards don't care. If one of them dies, they die. I would never have believed our country, the country we all fought for, could set up camps like these to put our citizens in. I always fought for freedom, and now our government has turned our citizens into slaves with no worth. When this is over, I might just move up to the mountains away from everything. I'm tired of what everybody calls progress."

The people came back out to work, and Gunman kept his eye on Jamie the rest of the day. Just before dark the prisoners were escorted to their barracks, and Pete and Gunman saw which one Jamie was in. The lights were on inside, and they saw which bunk she went to. The two watched as the guards padlocked the doors and stood outside the buildings. Later that night when everything was quiet, the guards put the dogs away and went to the front gate to talk. Pete and Gunman left silently as if they were ghosts.

Once at their hotel, Gunman sat at the small round table in their room and drew a map of the path they would take. "We'll go in this gate," he told Pete. "I haven't seen one person use this opening, so we should be safe. There's a lock on it, but I have the tools to open it. We'll wait until about three in the morning. The guards will still be by the main gate telling their stories and relaxing, and that's when we go in and get her. I didn't see anyone guarding from the inside, so we'll sneak in, grab Jamie, and leave. They won't know she is gone for several hours, so we should be home by then. Be careful no one inside sees you. They'll squeal as loud as they can to turn us in to get a break. They won't get one, but they don't know that."

Neither of them got any sleep, and they were dressed in their camouflage and had blackened their faces by one in the morning. By two-thirty the two were watching the guards from the brush. The guard dogs were put in their kennels, and the guards on patrol were at the main gate. Gunman and Pete slowly made their way to the entrance they would go through. As Gunman picked the lock and slowly opened the gate, they both heard a low growl. A dog's kennel door had not been shut, and he was out watching as he was trained to do. Quickly, Pete grabbed a sandwich he had in his knapsack and threw it into the kennel. The dog ran after the meat, and Gunman swiftly followed and shut the gate behind him leaving the dog inside to eat the food.

They both stood still for a moment making certain no one had heard or seen them. When they were sure they were in the clear, they headed for Jamie. Once again, Gunman picked the lock on the door, and the two entered the barrack silently.

Pete stood guard by the door, and Gunman went down close to the floor. Without a sound, he got to her bunk, stood up quickly, and put his hand over Jamie's mouth. He grabbed her tightly so she couldn't make any noise, and he looked in her face until she recognized him. He felt her body relax, and he picked her up off the bunk. Quickly they went out the door and back through the small gate they had entered. Gunman carried Jamie up to the brush while Pete stayed a little behind making sure no one was coming after them.

Once Gunman put Jamie down, she hugged him and started to cry. "Shh," he told her. The three hiked back to their car and left for home.

It was now the third of July. People had swamped the city by the thousands, and now there were more than three million people in D.C. ready to protest the evil government that had taken over.

Gregg was in contact with the head of each group around town. There had indeed been trouble, but the vets had put the agitators down quickly, and the march stayed peaceful. The city was so clogged with citizens who wanted their rights back, that marching down a street wasn't necessary. The Capitol, White House, Supreme Court, and Pentagon were surrounded by hundreds of thousands, and the people inside the buildings hadn't been able to leave for several days.

Gregg, Max, Mark, and people nearby began to erect a platform and podium for him to speak from. "I wonder where Gunman and Pete are?" he looked at Max. "They should be back by now. I hope nothing went wrong."

"They're fine," Max told his friend. "You know Gunman, he has to make certain he knows exactly what he's getting into before he'll move. Come on let's finish this stuff. By tomorrow we'll be ready to present our demands. I think the politicians and rich people in town know we mean business, and we aren't leaving until we get those resignations."

Gregg checked in with the heads of the groups, and every one of them sounded positive and certain the next day would be the right time to let the government know they were through.

It was very hard to navigate through the city with so many people, tents, and sleeping bags everywhere. Gunman, Pete, and Jamie headed toward the Capitol to try and find Gregg. It was dark before they got to the place they thought he would be, but they couldn't find him in the mass of people. Suddenly, Gunman saw Gregg get up on the platform to adjust something, and he grabbed Jamie's arm to take her to her husband.

Gregg was unaware they were there until he jumped down and turned to see them. He stood there for a second not comprehending what was going on. Then he smiled and grabbed Jamie hugging her as tightly as he could. He couldn't believe she was back. "Thank you, Gunman," he told his friend with tears in his eyes. Looking at Jamie, he told her he loved her.

"Okay," Gunman said. "We've got work to do. I'll take Jamie, and we'll find Jody. You keep busy," he looked at Gregg.

Everything was working out better than they planned. Pete had disappeared for a little while, and when he reappeared, he told Gregg, "Richard has friends who have set up some cameras around the country, and they are going to broadcast to the public what is happening at some of the state capitols and help broadcast what is happening in D.C. Many of the capitols around the country have masses of people marching around them too. We've also got screens up around D.C. so everyone can see why they are here and the results we are getting. This is a nationwide event buddy, and most of the citizens are supporting you."

Richard walked up, "We may get cut off by the regime, but our people have ways of getting around the establishment. They will try everything to stop us, but we aren't going to let that happen."

"Thanks, you two," Mark said. "It's people like you who are going to make this protest work."

"Thank you all," Gregg spoke loudly so those around could hear. "This has turned out because of all of the hard work everyone has done. Tomorrow we will make our demands, and we won't be backing down until our citizens have retaken our government and our freedom."

CHAPTER THIRTEEN

Inside the White House, Peterson was listening to one of his advisors. "Sir, the mass of people around D.C. is so large there is no way we can control their movement. We found the group who started this, but there are too many supporters around them. We are afraid if we go near the leaders it will cause a riot, and our people would be hurt if not killed. We have reports that many of the state capitols around the nation are also being mobbed by citizens who are angry about the laws that have been made. This seems to be a nationwide march with no end in sight."

"I don't care about the state capitols. Concentrate on D.C. Use tear gas, and start from the outside and pull people out of the crowd. Throw them in jail. Our military is on the perimeter of the White House, Capitol, Supreme Court, and Pentagon, so they can shoot any disrupters. We have to get this under control now!" Jacob insisted. "I also want to see any tape you have on this uncontrolled mob. We are going to prosecute every last one of them!"

The next day, the crowd was ready for the upcoming speech. More and more citizens choked the city, and flags were held high by people dressed in red, white, and blue. The screens around town showed the marchers at different state capitols as well as those in D.C. Excitement penetrated the air, and everyone was ready to take back what belonged to them.

Pete started yelling to the masses, "If you can't see a screen, you can see what is happening on the App 'Rights'. Download it and stream 'Rights' videos." The crowd repeated the message, and it was like a wave that carried the information around D.C. In no time at all, every eye was on a screen or on a cell phone watching.

Each individual was aware that it was the fourth of July and was ecstatic that this historical event was happening on the same day that our Founding Fathers declared independence.

Gregg mounted the platform and stood at the podium motionless for a minute before he started. People across the nation waited breathlessly to see what he was going to say and what they could expect for their future and that of upcoming generations.

He began, "Thank you, everyone, for coming here to stand strong for freedom." The crowd roared.

"I and millions of our citizens from across the nation stand before our government this day in protest of the actions our Executive Administration, Congress, Judicial system and government agency heads have taken without the consent of the people. We, the citizens of this great nation, borrow a portion of the wisdom our Founding Fathers set in the *'Declaration of Independence'* to proclaim to this corrupt and evil government that we will no longer stand for the tyranny you offer.

As the *'Declaration of Independence'* states, *'We hold these truths to be self-evident, that all men are created equal, that they are endowed by their Creator with certain unalienable Rights, that among these are Life, Liberty, and the pursuit of Happiness.--That to secure these rights, Governments are instituted among Men, deriving their just powers from the consent of the governed.--That whenever any Form of Government becomes destructive of these ends, it is the Right of the People to alter or to abolish it, and to institute new Government, laying its foundation on such principles and organizing its powers in such form, as to them shall seem most likely to effect their Safety and Happiness. Prudence, indeed, will dictate that Governments long established should not be changed for light and transient causes; and accordingly all experience hath shewn, that mankind are more disposed to suffer, while evils are sufferable, than to right themselves by abolishing the forms to which they are accustomed. But when a long train of abuses and usurpations, pursuing invariably the same Object evinces a design to reduce them under absolute Despotism, it is their right, it is their duty, to throw off such Government, and to provide new Guards for their future security.'*

As our Founding Fathers saw a government of their time that cared nothing for the people, we now see the same in our government. We find ourselves in a situation where the people are abused and government is the abuser. Instead of dealing with a callous dictator, we now are being berated, degraded, and victims of multiple tyrants who are positioned across our leadership. People who are power hungry, thirsty for wealth beyond any fortune they could actually spend or use, and desirous of top status worldwide.

These same people and their followers have seeded our education system, laws, and all media with immoral ideals to encourage our society to rid itself of the God we trust and to instill immoral behavior throughout our culture. Politicians have worked hard to purge our society of a family-oriented nucleus and have encouraged many in our country to disregard law and family allegiance by turning to violence, crime, drug addiction, and the development of a society that believes immorality and individualism are the new religions.

I stand before you today to remind you that we are Americans, and we are loyal to the principles of God, Family, Country, in that order, which we live by and expect our official representatives to function by. Our leaders are put on notice this very moment that our citizens will no longer stand for your greedy, selfish, immoral behavior.

This country thanked our Creator for all of His assistance in guiding us to freedom during the Revolutionary War. We have lived by God's laws and morals for centuries, and now you believe that you can wipe that away and place yourselves on pedestals as our liberators by confusion, contradiction, illogical reasoning, and insisting we follow what you have chosen for us. Millions of people have come to our nation's capital, and many millions more have congregated across the nation to demand a change of governance.

Our country was built on decency and laws to protect our citizens. Instead, we now see our children taken, our land and assets confiscated, and our homes invaded. Rather than protect citizens, our politicians allow our people to be harassed, jailed, and held without due process by government agencies overstepping their authority. We watch judicial courts refuse to hear cases that are critical to the progress and stability of our country. Many judges hearing cases often ignore the rights of citizens while criminals are set free to prey on others.

Many politicians focus actions on personal gain by spending taxpayer dollars on lobbyist desires disregarding what their people need, selling out their homeland to foreigners, and taking away our country's capabilities so foreign countries can seize control of our food supply, energy, and provide a larger and deadlier military for their benefit.

For years, we have found proof of officials who have worked with foreign governments to gain compensation through underhanded business deals or gaining wealth by selling access to officials, land, resources, and technology to the detriment of our country. We now have foreign military holding power over our citizens and foreign interests building, farming, and running industry on our land. No United States bureaucrat outcry or resistance has been forthcoming.

Our federal government exists to protect each state from invasion, and as of today with the consent of many United States government officials, citizens have been invaded by illegal immigrants who have caused an increase in diseases, an exponential rise in drug dealing and drug overdose, an increase in murders of our citizens, a huge growth in crime, and a large surge of attacks on our citizens on our own streets. These same illegal immigrants have overburdened our housing, roads, transportation systems, education system, and tax monies used to support them. Now, our homes have been opened by United States officials, and our citizens have been made to harbor people who are in our country illegally.

Many of our leaders have encouraged the tremendous crime that our citizens must deal with in their daily lives while turning a blind eye to punishing the culprits. While this goes on, government officials hire security details to protect themselves and build walls around their homes at the peoples' expense. Money spent on the rogue regime that looks down on our citizens and cares nothing for their safety.

While our people have had their rights taken away, parents watch as their children have been moved to government schools under federal supervision to teach them all of the immorality that is apparent in society. The parents have no say in the education their children receive. This government believes they will take over management of our kids and train them to obey on command.

We are given meaningless jobs that must be performed so we can eat while the commodities we produce are used by foreign countries on our land or overseas to advance foreign wealth, technology, education, and military capabilities. For our hard work, we are given credit at the discretion of the Administration for a month's work to buy unsatisfactory food and other needed product.

Many officials have insisted our citizens' guns be taken away, our people be spied on, and our citizens be imprisoned for utilizing free speech without due process. To keep people in line, these same leaders ensure propaganda is reported on government run media making certain many people stay unaware of the devious behavior of our government officials and agencies.

The 'new order' many in the regime practice has changed critical elements of our everyday living without allowing our citizens to vote on the very issues that alter our country's function and way forward. These same officials disregard citizens' questions and demands for different action.

Most of the official representatives and agency officials we have spoken about have overstepped their authority and have been sucking the blood out of its citizens long enough. You now tell us who we can marry and if we can marry, if we can or cannot travel, and how warm or cool we are allowed to keep our homes. You have lied to your people about the bombings and the radiation emitted from the bombing of our nation, and we have recordings from corrupt officials stating they will sell our children as slaves and not allow seniors medicine.

This rogue regime now takes those who disagree with its edicts to labor or rebel camps and has no qualms over killing our people for non-valid reasons. You have stripped our great country of its republic of the people, by the people, and for the people and have made our country a communist dictatorship forcing life, liberty, and the pursuit of happiness as ideals of the past.

We have documented proof from a current senator and a retired congressman that many of our elected officials have disregarded our Constitution, the very law they take an oath to uphold. Many laws are also ignored by multiple officials, and any pursuit of justice to hold these individuals accountable has been ignored by the 'Old Guard' who have sat in official seats for far too many years. This same 'Old Guard' now believes they are no longer public servants but dictators and our citizens are their menial servants.

No accountability is seen for these infractions. Many unrealistic committees are formed to investigate anyone who does not follow the rogue officials while allowing these same officials to break the law, abandon the welfare of the citizens, and work for the destruction of our democracy.

It is not alright for the forestated issues to be pushed on our people. No longer will citizens be subjects to elected or appointed oppressors. Because of the breaches discussed and others as well, the people of the United States are declaring their freedom from the debilitating government in power."

The crowds cheered so loudly in D.C. it was deafening. The screens that had been set up showed millions of people across the nation at their state capitols cheering and waving flags.

While Gregg waited for the crowd to quiet down, a group of FBI agents walked up to the platform stairs. Some of the men in the crowd saw them and moved to the steps above them blocking their path. "What do you want?" one of the men asked the agents.

"We're FBI agents," and one of them flipped their badge up for the men to see. "Move aside, you're interfering in government business."

"You don't have any business here," one of the men said as he refused to move. "This is a citizens' march and you're not invited."

"We need to arrest the man at the podium," one of the agents insisted.

"You aren't going to arrest anyone," another man said. "Now move along, because you're not welcome here."

The agents knew they weren't going to be able to get to Gregg, so they stepped back and called to one of the sergeants who was over the troops standing nearby. In a few minutes, military members surrounded the platform and pushed the people back who were close by. As the agents went towards the platform, the men slid past the soldiers and stood in front of them telling them to go away. No one moved for a full minute, and then the people started shifting in towards the platform past the military to block the FBI while they were yelling for the agents to move away. The FBI stepped back and didn't know what to do, so they decided to wait until they could approach another way.

Gregg began again, "We understand that there are a few good people in the leadership of our country who work hard for the United States citizens. Unfortunately, in every party and agency the corruption is so intertwined within and so ingrained in everyday actions that it would be impossible to clean out the corruption without a complete refreshing of the entire top layer of government. Because of all of this, we are forced to demand the following and will not disband until our requirements have been met.

We demand resignations from everyone in the White House Administration including all staffers. We require resignations from every person in the Legislative Branch and their staffers."

The crowd roared with approval. They started to chant 'resign, resign', and Gregg waited while the people expressed their frustrations and pleasure of finally getting a say in what their government would do.

Gregg was finally able to continue, "We demand the resignation of the Supreme Court Justices, their staff members, and all elected and appointed judges. We also require that the top officials in the Pentagon and their staff as well as all heads of federal agencies from GS-15 and above resign."

Again, the crowd went wild. The people protesting across the nation were backing Gregg one hundred percent and were elated to be standing up to the despotic government that had grown over decades.

"To remedy these vacancies," Gregg went on once the cheering died down, "persons of integrity have been chosen by the people and will be asked to serve in strategic positions immediately. The lower-level people in government will continue doing the hard work of keeping our country moving along without interference from tyrannical bosses.

As soon as possible, we will hold honest elections with paper ballots made out by our citizens at the polling locations, and mail-in ballots will only be used by those not able to go to the polls and who have confirmed this before the election. Once installed, the new Congress will ensure new amendments to the Constitution are proposed stating term and age limits for all of Congress, the Supreme Court Justices, and all judges. From that point on, the people will elect Supreme Court Justices and all judges not previously voted in by the people. The president will have an upper and lower age limit.

The people will reclaim the assets taken from us, and we will have our homes returned to us as our individual family dwellings. Our country will once again become energy independent and run private businesses, and we will build this nation into a powerhouse by manufacturing our own goods and selling to the rest of the world.

Foreign business will be removed from our nation, and all land and buildings in our country owned by foreign countries or foreign citizens will be returned and be United States property.

We will cut the fat out of the government that has enlarged exponentially over the decades, and we will return most programs and services back to the states or to the people instead of allowing the federal government to oversee them.

Every government official who has evidence against them of wrong doing will be investigated and prosecuted for appropriate crimes. You will be held accountable for your actions or lack of actions that have so hurt our society.

We will continue to run our country by looking to God for guidance and blessings, and the good of the United States will be our focus while we continue to assist those worldwide who need our help. We will prosper through a capitalist society and provide opportunity to those who wish to follow the law and achieve.

All current and future government officials are now put on notice that the people will no longer be submissive to, spied on, or run by politicians or the rich of the business world. The United States is again a country of the people, by the people, and for the people!"

Gregg turned from the podium and the people were laughing and slapping each other on the back. A wave of thankfulness went over all as they understood their country was going to be reborn and taken back from oppression.

Jacob watched the speech from the White House. "How are they transmitting to the screens around town and to the capitols around the nation? I told you this was not to be shown or heard anywhere in the country, so how did this happen?" he asked Dick, the FBI agent, and the advisor who stood before him.

"I don't know how they did this," the FBI agent told him. "They must have contacts across the country who agreed to air this outside of the normal media channels we control."

"Well find out how they did it and stop it!" Jacob pounded his fist on his desk. "All of you have bungled this so badly, so you better fix it." He was so angry he waved them out of the room so he could calm down.

A little while later, they were called back into his office. "That bastard will regret the day he started this. I want the military to arrest him and anyone who is standing close to him."

Lucy walked into the room while he was talking and spoke softly to him, "Do you think that is smart right now? Maybe we should wait until the cheers die down."

Jacob looked at her and seemed to quiet down a bit, "You're right, that will only incite the crowd. So, after dark sharp shooters will take that bastard out. We'll plant people in the crowd to start trouble, and it will look like the unrest caused his death. I also want the military to start disbanding these people now. Soldiers can group together and take a section at a time. I want them gone so the people get back to the way they were working before. This has to end now."

The advisor found enough courage to address his boss, "That's going to take some time, sir. Maybe it would be better to send a negotiator out to them and promise them meetings about their concerns if they tell the crowds to go home."

Lucy nodded, "Let's try that, Jacob. We'll take it step by step to deescalate the situation. If we overreact, this disorder will only get worse and they will only dig in their heels harder."

"Alright," Jacob scowled, "bring that son-of-a-bitch in and his main buddies. After a few days of discussion, we'll throw their asses in jail. I call this treason."

Two special agents, Ben and Drew, trained in negotiations were sent out into the crowd to talk to Gregg. Mark, Max, and Gunman stood near Gregg watching for trouble.

Ben approached Gregg, and Gunman stood in front of him. "Excuse me sir, I would like to talk to the speaker who just gave that speech a little while ago.

"What do you want to talk about?" Gunman stood firm and kept constant eye contact with Ben.

141

"It's official business, sir," Ben stood firm as well keeping his gaze steady and not backing down.

"Gregg," Gunman said without moving, "this guy wants to talk to you. He's from Peterson I think."

Gregg turned around and walked over to Gunman. He stood there waiting for Ben to speak.

"Sir," Ben said to Gregg, "the President would like to negotiate with you on your demands."

Gregg smiled at the man sent in to crush the protest of millions of people, "No negotiations. We want results now, and you can go back and tell Peterson that we are not leaving this city until we have the resignations we demand."

"It is in everyone's interest to talk this through and come to a consensus," Ben stood firm.

"Our current government continues to harm our citizens. There will be no negotiations."

Ben and Gregg had a stare down. Gregg won, and Ben joined Drew to go back and report what happened. Back in Jacob's office, Ben told Peterson Gregg's answer. "Sir, we spoke with the man who delivered the speech. He refused to negotiate." Jacob sent them out of the room.

All the people in the White House were in the hallways talking and wondering what Jacob was going to do about this. They all saw the speech, and they could see the masses across the city.

"Jacob," Lucy looked upset, "they're all asking what is going to be done about this. Everyone is afraid, and no one is going to resign. We are at a very scary stalemate."

"That bastard is going to pay for this," he answered her. "Get the Chairman of the Joint Chiefs back in here."

Dick walked back into Jacob's office, "Yes, sir."

Jacob was beyond upset, "You are going to order a few of your soldiers to fire into the crowd. That should disperse everyone, and I want the leader who gave the speech killed."

"Sir," Dick looked very concerned, "if I do that, many of our citizens will be killed."

"I don't give a damn," Jacob stood up. "I want this taken care of. They are traitors to our country and must be dealt with."

The Chairman stood there for a minute not really knowing what to do. Then he saluted and turned to leave the room. Once outside of the office, he motioned to a Lieutenant Colonel who was standing nearby. The General told him what he wanted the troops by the Capitol to do, and the subordinate gave a salute and walked away.

The Lieutenant Colonel went outside and walked over to a sergeant standing nearby. He asked to use his military phone. A sergeant who had his troops by the Capitol answered the call, so the Lieutenant Colonel told him to let his troops know they would fire when ordered to. They were to kill the leader who gave the speech, and the rest were to fire in the air as warning shots.

The troops by the platform at the Capitol received their orders and lifted their rifles ready to shoot. The sergeant gave the order, and the troops fired. Gunman saw them raise their guns, and just as they fired at Gregg, Gunman moved in front of him. He fell to the ground mortally wounded. Hundreds of warning shots went off at the same time, and the crowd became very quiet.

Gregg knelt down by his friend and started to cry. Mark and Max were there instantly and couldn't believe what Gunman had done. "He did that for our country," Mark said with tears in his eyes grasping Gregg's shoulder. "He wouldn't have wanted to die any other way." Anger went through Gregg like he had never felt before. He knew this regime would continue killing innocent people, and he was there to ensure this would stop. He got back on the platform and started chanting, "Resign, resign."

The people did not scatter like Jacob thought they would. They stayed where they were determined that the corrupt regime would end and they would regain their country. They started chanting with Gregg, "Resign, resign."

The Lieutenant Colonel could see on a screen from the White House what had happened. He radioed for the sergeant to fire again. When their superior gave another order to fire, the troops lowered their weapons to their sides. One by one, the soldiers put the butt of their guns on the ground and joined the crowd by turning to face the Capitol. As word spread, the troops around the city did the same. They all joined the people by turning to look at the Capitol, White House, Supreme Court, and Pentagon. No matter what they were ordered to do, they stood fast with the people knowing that they were serving their country by upholding the oath they took when they entered the Service. Each one of them believed that to uphold the Constitution they couldn't support the regime that had taken hold of the country. The top level of government had become domestic terrorists, and to protect the people and ensure their oaths were honored, they had to refuse to go against the Constitution any further.

Everyone in government saw the military change sides and knew the support system they relied on was finished. Jacob called the foreign military leaders and told them to bring their troops to the White House. "If they think I'm done, they're wrong," Jacob muttered to himself.

In a matter of a few minutes, trucks of foreign military pulled up by the White House gate, and troops jumped out. They were carrying assault weapons, and they pushed the guards at the gate out of the way. The foreign soldiers drove directly up the avenue to the White House and waited outside guarding the structure while their superior officer went in.

Just as the foreign officer arrived in Jacob's office, the Chairman of the Joint Chiefs stepped back into the room. Peterson gave the foreign general orders to go out in the crowds and fire randomly killing citizens as a warning, and he wanted the speaker at the event shot. As the foreign officer saluted and turned, Dick stood in the doorway blocking his exit. "I wouldn't do that if I were you, sir," he told the President.

"Jacob looked stunned, "Who are you to tell me what to do?" Jacob was furious.

"Our soldiers aren't going to let the foreign troops fire on our citizens. My soldiers will fight to the death to protect them, and as you saw, my troops turned from holding our people back to joining them. I'm afraid we are going to have to place you in a safe location until it is determined what action can be taken against your order to fire on our people. As of this moment, you are no longer presiding over our military. We will leave it up to the courts and the prosecutors as to what action should be taken against you. Of course if you resign, the penalty might be lessened.

"Senator Seagly stepped into his office holding a stack of papers. "This is your fault, Jacob, for what you've done to our citizens and our country. Here is my resignation, and here is a form for you to sign that you are stepping down from your duties. I suggest you sign it."

Jacob took the document and looked out of a window at the crowd. He glanced out his office door and saw people standing in the hallway looking to him for an answer. They all knew the mass of people were not going to leave until they got written compliance from everyone they named. Jacob crumpled the paper and threw it on the floor.

Seagly walked out of Peterson's office and out of the White House. He continued down to the crowd and handed them his resignation. "You're brave Americans, and I know you did the right thing."

One of the people who had a bike took the signed acknowledgement of defeat over to Gregg outside the Capitol. Pete was still filming, and everyone saw on the screens that the resignations had begun. Cheering started and continued as more and more of the elected and nominated people handed in their signed surrender. The ones who held off looked at each other knowing it was a losing battle and eventually they would be thrown out of the government as well.

The Chairman of the Joint Chiefs called his Lieutenant Colonel into the room and told him to take Jacob to a safe site. "Put this man under surveillance. We will ensure due process unlike the treatment our people received." Peterson had no choice but to go with the officer.

Once the news came out, the people were jubilant, and Gregg got back on the platform. "We will continue to stay until we have resignations from all of the officials and nominated people who must leave office now. Because of the good people in this country, we are set on a path to restore our government and turn it back into the great republic it was years ago. From this day forth, our country again belongs to the people, and anyone who decides to function outside of the law will be held accountable. Finally, after a decade of abuse, our citizens will regain their freedom. I am asking that the following people who are trusted and have proven themselves to be patriots will work with us to refresh this government." He read off a list of names many of the group organizers in the crowd had nominated. These were very respected people who Gregg hoped would join them to begin the process of altering their government to give the power back to the people.

Over the following months, hundreds of officials and appointees were charged with crimes against the people. They were all arrested and were put in ordinary jails to await their trials. Citizens started to see justice as it was meant to be in the great nation of the United States of America.

www.ingramcontent.com/pod-product-compliance
Lightning Source LLC
Chambersburg PA
CBHW021127020426
42331CB00005B/656